OMC SMOKEHOUSE
· DULUTH, MN ·
COOKBOOK

OMC SMOKEHOUSE

• DULUTH, MN •

COOKBOOK

WRITTEN BY **ROBERT LILLEGARD**

PHOTOGRAPHY BY **ROLF HAGBERG**

Duluth Grill Publishing
118 South 27th Avenue West
Duluth, MN 55806
218-726-1150
info@DuluthGrill.com

OMC Smokehouse Cookbook

Printed in the United States of America
10 9 8 7 6 5 4 3 2 1 0 First Edition

ISBN: 978-0-9886112-2-1

All photos by Rolf Hagberg except where otherwise noted.
Designed by Kollath Graphic Design

CONTENTS

List of Recipes ii

A Word from Louis iv

Dedication & Author's Note v

What Is Barbecue? 1

Perfect Vs. Good Enough 4

Rubs 5

What's in a Name? Why "OMC"? 8

Barbecue Sauces 9

Sauces & Dressings 13

Northern Hospitality 18

Sides 21

Pickles 31

"We'll Never Open A Restaurant Again" 33

Appetizers 37

*Thousands of Miles, Tens of Thousands of Calories,
and One Cramped Car* 43

Oink
How to 48
Recipes 57

Moo
How to 63
Recipes 68

Cluck
How to 75
Recipes 81

Pretending You Can't Walk, Slashed Tires, and Raising Kids 87

Other Proteins
How to 89
Recipes 92

Cocktails 97

The Right Meat 105

Baked Goods & Desserts 107

What Makes a Good Home Smoker? 113

What Makes Good Smoking Wood? 116

Acknowledgments 117

Index 119

LIST OF RECIPES

Rubs

Catfish Rub 6

Pork Rub. 6

Chicken Rub. 6

Nashville Hot Chicken Rub. 7

Brisket Rub. 7

Burger Seasoning 7

"Larry's" Seasoning Salt 7

Barbecue Sauces

Honey Barbecue Sauce 10

Alabama White Sauce 10

Georgia Gold 10

14° ESB Barbecue Sauce 11

Chipotle Cilantro Barbecue Sauce. 11

Tomato and Black Pepper Jam 12

Korean Barbecue Sauce 12

Sauces and Dressings

Rhubarb and Cranberry Jam 14

Balsamic Dressing 14

Blue Cheese Dressing. 14

French Dressing 15

Ranch Dressing 15

Malt Vinegar Aioli 15

Soba Noodle Dressing 16

Hot Brown Gravy 16

Jalapeño Business 16

Cheese Sauce 17

Country Gravy 17

Sides

OMC Beans 22

Collard Greens. 22

Classic Coleslaw 23

Elotes 23

Cheesy Jalapeño Grits 24

Candied Sweet Potato Bake 25

Bacon and Bleu Cheese Potato Salad . . . 26

Peas and Pancetta 27

Jalapeño Lime Slaw 28

Haystack Onions 28

French Fries. 29

Corn Relish. 30

Pickles

Brined Onions 31

Pickled Jalapeños. 32

Appetizers

Super Nachos 38

Smoked Chicken Quesadilla 39

Jalapeño Brisket Bombs 40

Pork Belly Lettuce Wraps 41

Salmon Pimento Dip. 42

Oink

Pork Butt 48

Pulled Pork. 51

St. Louis Style Pork Ribs. 53

Cured, Braised, Smoked, and
   Fried Pork Belly. 55

Pork n' Grits 57

Smoked Pork Burrito Bowl 58

Northern Pride 59

Korean BBQ Pork Belly Sandwich 60

Zip A Dee Do Da 61

Korean BBQ Pork Belly Soba
    Noodle Bow 62

Spicy Boiled Pecans 62

Moo

Brisket 64

Loaded Mac and Cheese 68

OMC Tacos 69

Brisket and Cheddar 70

Haystack Brisket 71

Bama Brisket Wrap 72

OMC Burger 73

Cluck

Chicken Marinade 76

Chicken Tender Dip and Dredge 77

Smoked Chicken Wings 79

Whole Smoked Chicken 80

BBQ Ranch Salad 81

Smoked Chicken Club Wrap 81

Henny Penny 82

Nashville Hot Chicken Sandwich 83

Georgia Gold Sandwich 84

Kentucky Hot Brown 85

Chicken/Turkey Stacker 85

Other Proteins

Smoked Salmon 90

Smoked Salmon Wrap 92

Fried Catfish 93

Catfish Sandwich 94

Vegetarian Sloppy Joe 95

Cocktails

Karin's Kup 98

Watermelon . . . . Gin 99

Old Fashioned 100

Margarita 101

Kentucky Gold Rush 102

Red Sangria 103

N/A Lemonade 104

Baked Goods and Desserts

Whoopie Pie 108

Toffee Bundt Cake 109

Salted Beer Caramel 109

Hummingbird Cake 110

Biscuits 111

Cornbread 112

A WORD FROM LOUIS

The OMC started out as an opportunity for us to rebuild the Lincoln Park neighborhood that we have been a part of since 2001 with the Duluth Grill. We thought: what better way to bring joy and excitement to the streets of Lincoln Park than Southern-inspired BBQ? Little did we know it would turn out to be much more than selling food and more about coming together with an amazing team over the years that helped shape the OMC to where it is today. Thank you to everyone that is and has been part of the journey. We hope you are as proud of this as we are to share it with you!

—Louis

The whole OMC gang From left to right, top to bottom:
Back row: **Dan LeFebvre holding Oakley, Chelsea Breimon, Ashley & Louie Hanson, Jaima & Tom Hanson, Tony Jansen, Valerie & Brad Bigelow, Julie & Jeff Petcoff and Caden Olson;**
Front row: **Gavin & Emmett Swanson, Willow LeFebvre, Parker & Peyton Hanson, Eliott & Ashley Bigelow and Corbin Petcoff.**

DEDICATION & AUTHOR'S NOTE

DEDICATION

This book is dedicated to Alicia, my favorite wife, who has been married to me for ten years and looks to be around for the long haul.

AUTHOR'S NOTE

The first good barbecue I had in Minnesota was at The Piggy in Walker, an extremely surprising find for a rural town of 1000. But when I learned the back story, I understood how classic southern food could end up so far north. The founder got bored after retirement, so he traveled south, got himself invited into a few kitchens, and asked barbecue cooks for advice until he could imitate their style.

The second great barbecue I had in Minnesota was at the OMC Smokehouse in Duluth. I've known Tom, Jaima, Louis, Jeff, and Dan since 2011, so I wasn't surprised to learn that they had taken their time to study barbecue "at the source". Through a series of pilgrimages to barbecue country, stints working in kitchens, and careful experimentation, they developed their own techniques and style. I think barbecue must be earned. I don't think it requires growing up in Texas or spending 30 years next to a pit, but I do think it requires respect. OMC respects barbecue. And we, in turn, should respect OMC.

I really enjoyed working on this cookbook. Whether you dabble with a sauce here and a side dish there or go all-in and smoke your own brisket, I hope it helps you bring the restaurant's flavors to your home.

—Robert

WHAT IS BARBECUE?

"Barbecue may not be the road to world peace, but it's a start."
—*Anthony Bourdain*

"**Barbecue is a party.** Barbecue is picnic tables, family gatherings, everyone being together. They cook all day, they cook all night. It's a planned event. You all have a good time just with music, talking, eating, sharing each other's barbecue stories and recipes."
—*Jaima Hanson*

"**The barbecue world is not a huge world.** People are connected. They've trained under each other and worked for each other, laughed together and cried together, celebrated Christmas together and attended each others' parents' funerals."
—*Tom Hanson*

"**Barbecue is an incredibly democratic food.** It's cheaper than McDonald's in many places and far more delicious."
—*Michael Pollan*

"**I didn't even smoke a brisket until we decided to open the OMC.** I figured I could travel and have people show me the culture of barbecue and why they do what they do. Why does one BBQ place have no one at it, and the next BBQ place has a line out the

door for two hours? Looking at the places that have been really packed, they care a lot about the outcome of how their product is produced every day. And they make it the same every single day. Consistency is key."

    —*Louis Hanson*

"A barbecue guy is not really so much a cook. He's a fire tender. He makes sure that it's consistent. The hardest part is finding people who are willing to stay with the fire for that long."

    —*Joe Slack*

"It's one thing to do a brisket for your friends, but we're doing 20 a day. After a while you get this inherent knowledge. If you cook a brisket three times, you'll cook it great once, once it will be okay, and once it will be a total failure. If you do it one hundred times you might have six failures, but you'll have a ton of big successes. A lot of it is touch and sight and feel, not recipe books. It's looking at a brisket and being able to say 'it needs a little longer'. You look at it and you can just tell."

    —*Tom Hanson*

"Barbecue is kind of a religion. Everyone down south is like 'mine's the best, mine's the best'. It's a respect factor. Everyone's anxious to enjoy it and have this camaraderie of family and fun. Home cooks can have a good time with it."

    —*Jaima Hanson*

"It definitely is that comfort food. It brings people from all over. In the Cities a lot of people would say 'have you been to OMC?' I'd say, 'yeah, I have'. It feels like home."

    —*Valerie Bigelow*

Perfect VS Good Enough

We don't want perfect to get in front of acceptable. Do you really want to brine, coat, and deep fry chicken to create chicken tenders? Sometimes the answer is yes—and we do that at the OMC—but we don't expect you to. Make a batch of Carolina Gold sauce and use store-bought chicken nuggets! Most of these recipes you can substitute ingredients or skip ones you don't have. The idea of barbecue is to take an idea and make it your own. This is how we do it, and what works for us, but feel free to modify it to your own blend.

One cool thing about this cookbook is that when you start, you start from scratch. But recipes build on each other and leftovers are always in style. Maybe you start with smoked pork and 14° ESB Mustard sauce. The next day you make some pickled onions and jalapeños to go with it. Then you make cheesy grits, which need the smoked pork and the pickled onions. Day four you want chicken tenders, so you add some honey to the 14° ESB Mustard sauce and get Georgia Gold. Day by day you're building a barbecue empire. Then you start getting into sandwiches and pretty soon you've opened your own food truck!

In this book we have tried to offer options to make things easier. One is to spread the work out over time. Our desserts freeze well, so freeze a batch of mini bundt cakes and take them out one by one as needed. You can make a big batch of any rub well in advance, or jar up some sauce to keep in the fridge for a while. And if you don't want to play bartender? Make a big pitcher or two of cocktails before the party and let guests help themselves. Several of our cocktails are already batch sized to make it easier to prep for a party.

In the how-to sections of Oink, Moo, and Cluck, you'll notice that we often make suggestions to simplify your life. We believe in smoking meat, but if you need to pick up something from the store? Make a homemade sauce and move on. Or maybe you want to make a grits bowl but only have some of the ingredients. That's when you swap out something else. Barbecue is about fun and trying your best, and sometimes the best you can do is take it one step at a time. **OMC**

RUBS

CATFISH
DREDGE

PORK RUB

CHICKEN
RUB

BRISKET
RUB

BURGER/
GRILL
SEASONING

HOT
NASHVILLE
CHICKEN
RUB

"LARRY'S"
SEASONING
SALT

Besides sauces, there are four main ways to get flavor into a piece of meat. You can rub, brine, inject, or smoke. The rub adds a flavor, bark and crispness. We also brine and smoke. Injecting can take hours or even days before you get the meat into the smoker. For a restaurant, and for many home cooks, that's too much time. Rubs are simple enough to throw together, they keep forever, and using them is fairly straightforward.

CATFISH DREDGE

A lot of fish is heavily breaded in the restaurant world. This rub, which can be used on walleye or sunfish too, is a mixture of all-purpose flour and cornmeal with a few spices. It's meant to be dredged right onto a piece of fish (no egg wash involved) and tossed directly into the fryer. That makes for a lighter fry which lets the fish's texture shine forth.

Yield:
2 Cups

Ingredients
1 cup all-purpose flour
1 cup cornmeal
2 Tbsp & 2 tsp salt
1/2 tsp cayenne
1 Tbsp black pepper
1½ tsp dill

Instructions
Combine all ingredients in a large container and mix well.

PORK RUB

This is a utilitarian rub and can be used on anything from butts to chops to ribs to chicken. But the OMC didn't want each meat to taste the same, so they called this a "pork rub". Over time, this rub will penetrate a large piece of meat. So you can put it on a pork butt and let it sit for two days before smoking, and it's really good. However, if you let it sit on ribs for a full day, it will cure the meat and make them too salty.

Yield:
6 Cups

Ingredients
1 lb sugar
1 cup sea salt
3/4 cup paprika
1/2 cup chili powder
1/2 cup black pepper
1/4 cup cumin
1/4 cup granulated garlic
1 Tbsp sage (dried)
1 Tbsp cinnamon

Instructions
Combine all ingredients in a large container and mix well.

CHICKEN RUB

Don't sprinkle this one on after cooking—it needs heat to develop. Thyme, sage, and onion bring up the flavors of Thanksgiving stuffing rather than being sweet/spicy like the basic pork rub. This can be used on other game birds, lamb or pork chops.

Yield:
3 Cups

Ingredients
1/2 cup onion powder
1 cup sea salt
1/2 cup granulated garlic
3 Tbsp & 1 tsp sage
3 Tbsp & 1 tsp paprika
3 Tbsp & 1 tsp thyme
3 Tbsp & 1 tsp black pepper

Instructions
Combine all ingredients in a large container and mix well.

NASHVILLE HOT CHICKEN RUB

Louis had Nashville hot chicken at the OMC that was so spicy it took him a year until he was willing to eat it again. He woke up at 4am, sweating, and thought "something is not right". "Maybe I'm just getting older, too," he muses. I (Robert) cried when I ate this chicken and it was only partially due to the heat. It was just a beautiful, beautiful dish. But be careful what you're signing up for!

Yield: 2 Cups

Ingredients
3/4 cup cayenne pepper
1/4 cup brown sugar
1 Tbsp black pepper
1 Tbsp salt
2 tsp paprika
2 tsp granulated garlic
2 cups heated sunflower oil
or lard

Instructions
This "rub" does not go on the chicken before frying: you actually turn it into a sauce. First, you dredge and fry the chicken the normal way (page 77). Then, you smear it with the Nashville Hot Chicken rub/sauce, made like this:

Combine all dry ingredients (everything but the oil or lard) in a large container or bowl and mix thoroughly. Heat lard or oil to 325°. Remove from heat and add seasoning. Stir well.

Use spoon or tongs to apply hot mixture to fried chicken. Remove from mixture and eat.

BRISKET RUB

There's nothing to say about brisket that hasn't already been said. It's a simple item, but it's so complex and challenging the OMC likes to leave it as close to natural as possible. Salt and pepper are called a Dalmatian rub in the barbecue world. A little mustard and pickle juice helps bind it together and stick to the brisket so it develops into a nice peppery bark.

Yield: 3 Cups

Ingredients
2 cups coarse ground pepper
3/4 cup kosher salt
1/2 cup smoked hot paprika

Instructions
Combine all ingredients in a large container and mix well.

BURGER SEASONING

A good simple burger is perfection. Use to taste, but we recommend 2 teaspoons per pound of ground beef.

Yield: 1 Cup

Ingredients
1/2 cup kosher salt
2 Tbsp & 1 tsp granulated garlic
2 Tbsp & 1 tsp onion powder

1/4 cup coarse pepper
1/4 cup Larry's seasoned salt

Instructions
Combine all ingredients in a large container and mix well.

"LARRY'S" SEASONING SALT

Most of you will probably buy seasoning salt, but it's really handy to have a "just in case" recipe if you run out. Another bonus of making it yourself is that you can tweak the ingredients. Love garlic? Add more. Not huge on turmeric? Cut it out. It's your party.

Yield: 2 Cups

Ingredients
1 cup sea salt
3 Tbsp & 3/4 tsp sugar

2 Tbsp & 2 tsp paprika
2 Tbsp & 2 tsp celery seed

Instructions
Combine all ingredients in a large container and mix well.

WHAT'S IN A NAME? WHY "OMC"?
Tom Hanson explains the story behind the restaurant's name

"I would walk to the Duluth Grill every day and think about different things in my head. I was thinking of acronyms. At first I was thinking '*WERF: West End Real Food.*' I would go into the restaurant and say 'what do you think about this?' I think we were doing a lot of West End stuff at the time. Bringing it back. Not to contradict the Lincoln Park thing, but to emphasize we're the west end of downtown. We're part of Duluth.

> "I said, 'uhhh...oink moo cluck.' The name kind of stuck and we went with it. People thought it was kind of funny."

Then, when I went on GoDaddy, *werf.com* was already taken. Every acronym I came up with people are like, 'mmmm... I don't know'. I said, 'what do you think about '*OMC Smokehouse*?' People said 'I like it! What does it mean?' I said, 'uhhh...oink moo cluck.' The name kind of stuck and we went with it. People thought it was kind of funny.

[The real story is that] I would go on and look up every GoDaddy name I could think of. I went on there and *OMCSmokehouse.com* wasn't taken.

Also, people like nicknames for restaurants, they kind of inherit them. The OMC Smokehouse is basically known around town as "The OMC".

And...who doesn't like that 90s one-hit wonder '*How Bizarre*'? The band who did that song was called OMC. That's destiny right there." OMC

Randomly thinking about stuff while you walk to work is the way a surprising amount of entrepreneurial activity gets done

BARBECUE SAUCES

HONEY
BARBECUE
SAUCE

ALABAMA
WHITE
SAUCE

14° ESB
BARBECUE
SAUCE

GEORGIA
GOLD

CHIPOTLE
CILANTRO
BARBECUE
SAUCE

KOREAN
BARBECUE
SAUCE

HONEY BARBECUE SAUCE

Yield:
3-4 Cups

In Minnesota we're not confined by a specific style of BBQ sauce. That lets us borrow from everywhere. This is a utility sauce—light, thin, zesty and sweet. It's not thick and sweet like Sweet Baby Ray's, it's more like a central Texas stovetop sauce. The OMC will place a 400 pound order of honey from Togo, MN to keep things local, but you   could also buy 400 pounds of honey for your house. Or not. Up to you.

Ingredients

15 oz tomato sauce
6 Tbsp honey
1/2 Cup red wine
   vinegar
1/2 Cup cider vinegar
4 Tbsp brown sugar
3 Tbsp yellow mustard
3 Tbsp lemon juice
2 Tbsp molasses
3 Tbsp Worcestershire

1 Tbsp sea salt
2 tsp minced garlic
1 tsp liquid smoke
1/2 tsp oregano
   (dried)
1/2 tsp chili
   powder
1/4 tsp black pepper

Instructions

Combine garlic and lemon juice in a blender until smooth. Add all ingredients to stock pot and bring to a boil.
   Reduce heat and simmer for 1/2 hour (sauce should be thin and zesty). Pour into storage containers and cool.

ALABAMA WHITE SAUCE

We love our ranch dressing in Minnesota. This is like the Southern version of that. This mayo-based sauce is a guilty pleasure down in Alabama. Scandinavians may find pepper too spicy, but horseradish is always okay for some reason! This sauce is the most used at the OMC.

Ingredients

Yield:
1½ Cups

1 Cup mayo
2½ Tbsp apple cider
   vinegar
2½ Tbsp prepared
   horseradish

1 Tbsp + 1 tsp honey
2 tsp fresh lemon juice
2 tsp prepared yellow
   mustard
1 tsp black pepper

1/2 tsp kosher salt
1/4 tsp cayenne
1/8 tsp granulated
   garlic

Instructions

Mix all ingredients in a bowl and whisk until creamy and smooth.

GEORGIA GOLD

Honey mustard—every child's favorite thing. When you amp up 14 ESB Mustard Sauce with extra honey, you make it more approachable while making your next batch of chicken nuggets sing.

Yield:
1¾ Cups

Ingredients

3/4 Cup 14° ESB BBQ Sauce (see following page)
1/2 Cup French's Yellow Mustard
1/2 Cup Honey

Instructions

Mix ingredients. See? Cooking can be easy.

14° ESB BARBECUE SAUCE

Down in the Carolinas mustard sauces are popular with pork. The OMC neighborhood has a lot of craft makers in it. Jeff helped develop this sauce based on Louis' favorite neighborhood beer, the Bent Paddle 14 Degree ESB. It gives it a nice bitterness.

**Yield:
3 Cups**

Ingredients

1½ Cups prepared
  yellow mustard
1/2 Cup brown sugar
3/4 Cup Bent Paddle
  14° ESB Beer (or other
  brown ale)
1 Tbsp chili powder
1/2 Cup apple cider
  vinegar

1 tsp ground black
  pepper
1 tsp ground white
  pepper
1/4 tsp cayenne pepper
1½ tsp Worcestershire
2 Tbsp butter
1½ tsp liquid smoke
1½ tsp Sriracha sauce

Instructions

In a medium sauce pot, add first 8 ingredients (mustard, brown sugar, apple cider vinegar, 14° ESB, chili powder, black pepper, white pepper, and cayenne pepper). Mix ingredients thoroughly and simmer for 20 minutes.

Add last 4 ingredients (Worcestershire sauce, butter, liquid smoke, and Sriracha sauce). Mix and simmer until butter melts fully. Turn off. Allow BBQ sauce to cool overnight in the refrigerator and enjoy.

CHIPOTLE CILANTRO BARBECUE SAUCE

When Louis was in Kansas City, a lot of sauces had fruit preserves like peaches or apricots in the sauce. Neither are very Minnesotan, but this state has more rhubarb than we know what to do with. If you leave your door unlocked at certain times of year, friends will literally leave unwanted rhubarb.

**Yield:
4 Cups**

Ingredients

2 Cups tomato sauce
1 Cup apple cider
  vinegar
1/4 cup chipotle peppers
  in adobo sauce
1/2 Cup brown sugar
1/2 Cup Rhubarb and
  Cranberry Jam
  (page 14)
1/4 Cup honey
2 Tbsp molasses
1/2 tsp liquid smoke
1¼ cup cilantro
  (finely chopped)

1 Tbsp lemon juice
1 Tbsp Worcestershire
1/2 Tbsp ground black
  pepper
1/2 Tbsp onion powder
1/2 Tbsp ground
  mustard

Instructions

In a blender, combine tomato sauce, apple cider vinegar, and chipotle peppers and blend until smooth. In large sauce pot combine all other ingredients (except cilantro). Bring sauce to a boil, then reduce heat to a simmer.

Simmer BBQ sauce for 1 hour, stir frequently. Remove BBQ sauce from heat and stir in fresh chopped cilantro.

South meets North — Spicy chipotle and tart rhubarb and cranberry are the core to this flavor.

**Chipotle Cilantro
Barbecue Sauce**

TOMATO AND ONION JAM

Louis' thought process was "how do you put all the best burger toppings in a single jam?" The mustard seeds add heat, there's sweetness from sugar, caramelized onions, and cooked down tomatoes. It makes a ready-to-go burger or works on other sandwiches too.

Yield: 4 Cups

Ingredients
3 cups crushed tomatoes
2 cups yellow onions (diced)
1/4 cup sugar
3 Tbsp honey
1 Tbsp lemon juice.
1/4 Tbsp minced garlic
1/2 tsp black pepper
1/2 tsp yellow mustard
    seed
1/4 tsp kosher salt
Enough oil to saute
    2 cups of onions
    (a couple tablespoons
    should be fine)

Instructions
Heat oil in a medium pot. When pan is hot, add onions and stir rapidly to ensure the onions do not burn. Once onions are in, reduce heat to low and allow the onion to caramelize for 5–10 min. (Onion should be translucent and golden brown).

Next add tomatoes, sugar, honey, lemon juice, minced garlic, black pepper, salt, and mustard seeds. Heat all ingredients together over medium heat, stirring frequently, until liquid is reduced to nothing and the mixture is a jam like consistency.

Remove mixture from pan and allow to cool. If you are looking for a smoother consistency, blend in a blender until the jam is well incorporated.

KOREAN BARBECUE SAUCE

There's more to BBQ than ribs, chicken and brisket. The OMC wanted to keep things interesting and fun so they took cues from Korea, another great barbecue nation. Tamari adds an umami richness, and ginger gives it a gentle fresh bite. It's a spicy sauce but not over the top, somewhere between Chipotle Cilantro and Nashville Hot.

Yield: 3 Cups

Ingredients
1 cup Sriracha
3/4 cup rice vinegar
3/4 cup tamari
    (soy sauce)
1/2 cup sugar

2½ Tbsp ground ginger
2¼ Tbsp garlic
    (granulated)
3 Tbsp lime juice
3 Tbsp sesame oil

Instructions
Blend everything (except sesame oil). With blender running on high, slowly add sesame oil. Store in fridge.

Korean
Barbecue
Sauce

SAUCES & DRESSINGS

BLEU
CHEESE
DRESSING

FRENCH
DRESSING

BALSAMIC
DRESSING

RANCH
DRESSING

RHUBARB AND CRANBERRY JAM

Don't run away! This is an icebox jam so you don't have to boil jars or anything. Louis invented this when it was time to come up with a fruit preserve for the chipotle sauce. This uses two Minnesota staples, cranberries and rhubarb. Tangy and sweet, this also accentuates the Jalapeño Brisket Bombs and the Turkey Stacker.

Ingredients
1 cup frozen rhubarb
1 cup frozen cranberries
1 cup organic cane sugar
1/4 cup apple juice

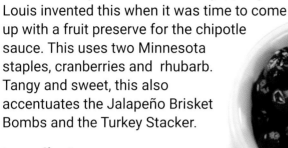

Jam texture should be smooth enough to squirt nicely out of your sauce bottle.

Yield: 2 Cups

Instructions
Place all ingredients in a medium sauce pan. Heat to a medium temperature and stir frequently. Stir until all ingredients are combined. Reduce heat to a simmer and cook until cranberries "pop". Mix in blender.

Rhubarb—We have over 200 rhubarb plants on site that we harvest.

BALSAMIC DRESSING

Sometimes you need a break from heavy barbecue food. Sometimes you need a break from recipes that take a long time to cook! This fits both bills—it's a quick and easy salad dressing to throw together when dinner needs to be on the table.

Yield: 2 Cups

Ingredients
1¾ cups olive oil
3/4 cups balsamic vinegar
1/4 cup red onion (diced)
1/2 tsp French's mustard

Instructions
Dice red onion. Mix vinegar, mustard, and red onion in blender. Blend until smooth.

Keeping the blender running slowly, add the oil and emulsify (it should take about a minute or two to add the oil).

BLUE CHEESE DRESSING

Big chunks of blue cheese makes this creamy and decadent! This is the famous recipe from the OMC's sister restaurant the Duluth Grill and has been in play there for over 10 years. This is a good accompaniment for chicken wings or a Nashville Hot Chicken sandwich.

Yield: 1½ Cups

Ingredients
1 Cup mayo
1/3 Cup blue cheese crumbles
4 Tbsp buttermilk
1 Tbsp grated Parmesan cheese
1/2 tsp granulated garlic
Dash of white pepper

Instructions
Place all ingredients in large mixing bowl. Whisk until fully incorporated (dressing should be chunky. *Do not* use a blender).

FRENCH DRESSING

Pungent, sweet, sour, and spicy. It's a classic French dressing with a little bit of an edge.

Yield: 3 Cups

Ingredients
1/2 cup diced red onion
1¼ cup olive oil
1 cup sugar
3/4 cup cider vinegar
1/4 cup ketchup
1 Tbsp balsamic
    vinegar
1/2 Tbsp salt
1/2 Tbsp mustard
1/2 Tbsp smokey
    paprika
1 tsp garlic powder
1 tsp celery seed

Instructions
In blender, blend onion and olive oil together until smooth. Add the rest of the ingredients and blend until smooth.

French
Dressing

Ranch
Dressing

RANCH DRESSING

Is this the best ranch in the Midwest? Even the OMC won't claim that—you'll have to decide for yourself. But it *is* homemade from scratch. It's not jarred and sitting on a shelf for four months; they pull the spices together just for this.

Yield: 3 Cups

Ingredients
2 cups mayo   1/2 Tbsp seasoned salt
1 cup buttermilk   1/4 Tbsp garlic powder
1 Tbsp parsley flakes   1/2 tsp onion powder
1/2 Tbsp black pepper   1/4 tsp thyme

Instructions
In a large mixing bowl, add mayo and seasonings and mix until smooth. Add buttermilk slowly while mixing and mix until smooth.

MALT VINEGAR AIOLI

It's a sweet, vinegary dill sauce meant to complement heavier fried dishes. Originally the OMC started out with duck fat fries. Since then they realized they're a BBQ restaurant and have a ton of extra beef fat left over. So they started rendering it and making tallow out of it to fry things in. Louis likes to ask "when you go to a restaurant, why get something you can make yourself at home? Try something different!" This is a sauce like that.

Yield: 2½ Cups

Ingredients
2 cups mayo   2 Tbsp French's
2 Tbsp malt vinegar   mustard
1/4 cup sugar   1 tsp kosher salt
1 Tbsp dill (dried)   1/2 tsp white pepper

Instructions
Add malt vinegar and sugar to large mixing bowl. Mix until sugar is dissolved. Add mayo, dill, mustard, kosher salt, and white pepper to malt vinegar and sugar mix. Blend until thoroughly mixed.

SOBA NOODLE DRESSING

With cold noodles you want a really powerful sauce. The OMC's is savory and umami rich. Why soba noodles at a barbecue place? Well, it does get hot in the summer...and sometimes you have one person at your table who just isn't feeling like a heavy dish. This is for that person.

Yield: 1½ Cups

Ingredients
1/2 cup Tamari
1/2 cup sesame
1/2 cup rice wine vinegar
2 Tbsp fish sauce
2 garlic cloves
1/2 tsp chili flakes

Instructions
Place all ingredients in a blender and blend until homogeneous.

HOT BROWN GRAVY

In spite of its name, this gravy is white rather than brown. This creamy Parmesan gravy with a little nutmeg is a classic with the Kentucky Hot Brown, an open-face turkey and tomato sandwich you'll find on page 85—but you could use it with a rotisserie chicken, on mashed potatoes, etc.

Yield: 1 Quart

Ingredients
Base
4 cups milk
3 oz Parmesan, freshly shredded
1/4 tsp nutmeg
1¼ tsp kosher salt
1¼ tsp black pepper
Roux
1/3 cup butter
1/3 cup flour

Instructions
Don't add your milk to the roux—that's how you get lumpy gravy! Instead, you'll make the roux first and then add it to the milk a bit at a time.
Roux: melt butter in a sauce pan, and then whisk in flour. Allow roux to cook until it develops a nutty aroma.
Base: In a saucepan, add milk, salt, pepper, and nutmeg. Turn heat on medium-high and stir in a teaspoon of roux at a time as milk heats up, whisking constantly. Heat until thickened. Turn heat off and stir in cheese.

JALAPEÑO BUSINESS

Reusing things is great. After making the jalapeño brisket bombs the OMC noticed they had the tops and insides of the jalapeños they were throwing away. Boil with vinegar and a little sugar. You can add it to collard greens, grits, or pork rinds for an extra kick.

Yield: 2 Cups

Ingredients
2 cups cider vinegar
1 cup jalapeño innards
3/4 cup sugar
1/4 cup onion scraps
2 garlic cloves

Save time? You can buy our Jalapeño Business at OMC (shameless self promotion)

Instructions
Bring to boil. Reduce to simmer. Reduce mixture by a third. Cool and place in fridge. Strain and remove scraps—liquid should be clear.

CHEESE SAUCE

When someone accuses the OMC of using Velveeta, which is not the case, Louis takes it as a compliment. Nothing melts like Velveeta! This handcrafted version goes with Mac and Cheese, Super Nachos, Burrito Bowls, or just drinking straight out of the bowl. Sodium citrate may sound scary, but it's non-GMO, gluten free, vegan, kosher, etc. Plus, it's necessary to make cheese sauce that stays smooth.

**Yield:
1 Quart**

Ingredients
1 lb shredded sharp
   cheddar
1 lb shredded smoked
   Gouda
3 cups 2% milk
1 Tbsp + 1 tsp sodium
   citrate
1 Tbsp salt
1½ tsp white vinegar
1/4 tsp Tabasco

Instructions
In a large stock pot, heat milk, sodium-citrate, salt, Tabasco, and white vinegar and bring to a simmer. Remove from heat and gradually add cheese, whisk until completely emulsified. Cool in fridge.

Gouda

Cheddar

COUNTRY GRAVY

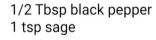

Biscuits and gravy. With homemade sausage, rendered bacon fat, this is a classic southern comfort food everyone can relate to, especially the morning after a long night Friday or Saturday.

**Yield:
1 Quart**

Ingredients
Roux
1/2 cup bacon grease
1/2 cup all purpose flour

Base
2 cups 2% milk
1½ cup water
1/4 lb sausage (raw)
1/2 Tbsp salt

1/2 Tbsp black pepper
1 tsp sage

Instructions
Base: Break apart sausage into smaller pieces. Brown sausage in a skillet. In a separate pot, add milk, water, black pepper, sage, and salt and bring to boil. Add browned sausage and drippings to pot.

Roux: In a separate skillet, heat bacon fat on medium heat. Once fat is hot, whisk in flour and cook for 2-4 minutes (roux should be smooth). Add roux to base one teaspoon at a time, whisking constantly, until the gravy thickens.

Northern Hospitality
HOW TO GET GOOD AT HOSTING

What does it mean to be a good host? The South is famous for its hospitality, but welcoming guests warmly has been a tradition for as long as humans have had homes. Tom Hanson calls his wife Jaima "the face and the voice of the front of the house". When you spend most of your waking moments working at the same restaurant, it's pretty important to make it a welcoming environment.

"We have this restaurant and it's like our home," Jaima says. "I want to make sure every person who comes through our doors feels like part of our restaurant."

Jaima's philosophy is "hungry, humble, smart and hospitalian". The first three come from a book Louis read called *The Ideal Team Player*. They have to do with food prep, and the art of cooking is why this book exists in the first place. But no one wants a good meal in terrible company. Jeff turned us on to Bobby Stuckey, the Colorado restaurateur who came up with the idea of "hospitalian". More than the act of service, it means making people feel good. Jaima doesn't like the gruff, no-nonsense serving philosophy you sometimes find at...you know the places.

"You have to treat people with respect and not be so quick to move on," Jaima says. "Stop, look, and listen to the guest, because without them we won't be here."

So how can you be a good host at your own barbecue?

"To be the most interesting person at a party you don't have to say much at all. Your ace-in-the-hole line: 'That's interesting! Tell me more.' You can draw people out quite quickly and learn their histories."

1. Trust your co-hosts

If you're teaming up with someone, like a spouse or a friend, find the tasks each of you enjoys most. Maybe you cook while they greet guests, or you take jackets and show guests the bathroom while they mix drinks. Getting along with your co-hosts goes a long way towards setting a tone.

"Customers say 'it's so fun to watch you guys. You're like dancing in and out of each other,'" Jaima says. "No one misses a beat because we all trust each other."

What about those stressful times—when the turkey's just out of the oven at Thanksgiving, or that 30 minute stretch right before the first guest walks in for a party?

"It's only for a short time—it comes and it goes and it's quick," Jaima says. "Work with your neighbor and help out."

2. Make your guests the center of attention

Everyone is the center of his or her own story. As a host, you find joy when you set your own anxieties aside for a night and just soak in your guests' worlds. Imagine their own epic sagas. Every person has a story, a battle, a quest. What drives them? What motivates them? What's on their mind during their week?

"I enjoy people. I enjoy hearing their stories and hearing them each and every day," Jaima says.

To be the most interesting person at a party you don't have to say much at all. Your ace-in-the-hole line: "That's interesting! Tell me more." You can draw people out quite quickly and learn their histories.

"Meeting people is a fun new event," Jaima says. "Moving and talking to people, watching them eat, and seeing the joy that comes across. It means a lot to me."

3. Put down your phone

A hard thing in the modern world! Try putting it in a basket in your room and shutting the door so you literally don't have the option of looking at it. Have you ever been to a restaurant where the hosts are talking among themselves? It's not a good feeling. Jaima's thought is that everybody should be acknowledged. In the restaurant industry, as in life, it helps to be a people person.

4. Remember the details

Before your guests come, think over your guest list and try to remember your last conversation. Was their son studying abroad? Did they pass a milestone at work? Do they always like their margarita a certain way? When they come, bring it into the conversation. Ask how Carson is liking his time in Sweden, congratulate them on the promotion, or just hand them that margarita with an extra twist of lime.

When people feel remembered, they feel cared for.

Jaima says she once had a customer pull her aside to share a story. The customer had overheard staff talking about a regular customer. Far from gossip or complaints, the staff was deeply concerned that they hadn't seen the regular in a while. Out of the thousands of people who pass through the restaurant monthly, the staff had noticed this one man's absence and they were really hoping he was okay.

"I just want to say what a lovely experience," the customer told Jaima. "I haven't had such a genuine experience like that ever before."

Reflecting on the story later, Jaima says it sums up a lot about hospitality.

"That may be why we're in the restaurant business," Jaima says. "It's kind of like an extended family here." OMC

> *"That may be why we're in the restaurant business,"* Jaima says. *"It's kind of like an extended family here."*

SIDES

From a rich potato salad with bacon and blue cheese that will make you the star at your next potluck to the grits that changed Louis forever; from zesty slaw to creamy Mexican grilled corn, these are dishes you could make any night of the week. You can't always find the time to smoke a big hunk of pork. But we have a feeling you'll find time for these.

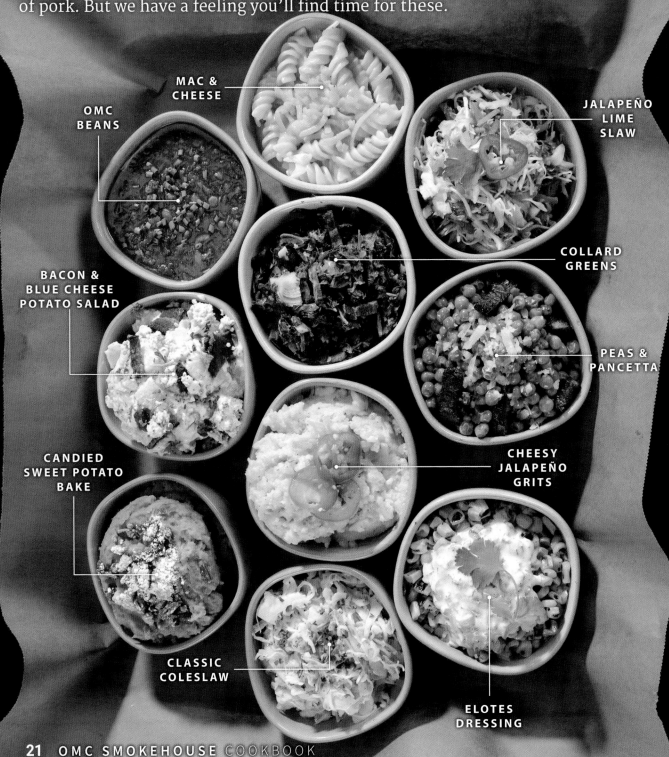

MAC & CHEESE

OMC BEANS

JALAPEÑO LIME SLAW

COLLARD GREENS

BACON & BLUE CHEESE POTATO SALAD

PEAS & PANCETTA

CANDIED SWEET POTATO BAKE

CHEESY JALAPEÑO GRITS

CLASSIC COLESLAW

ELOTES DRESSING

OMC BEANS

Baked beans with brown sugar are delicious, but these are not those. First the OMC experimented with rich French *cassoulet* style beans, which were delicious but way too labor intensive. Then they tried a butter bean and corn dish using lima beans. These were one of Louis' favorite, but "lima beans" can be a tough sell. Finally, the kitchen managers landed on a chili-forward interpretation of the classic brown sugar baked navy beans. It has the same beans and similar savory notes, but with extra spice instead of the sugar.

Yield: 2 Quarts

Ingredients

1 lb dried navy beans
2 cup yellow onions, diced
1/3 cup celery, diced
1½ Tbsp garlic cloves, minced
1 Tbsp cumin
1 Tbsp smoked paprika
3/4 tsp pepper
1½ Tbsp kosher salt
1 tsp ground Guajillo pepper
1 tsp oregano (dried)

2½ oz chicken, smoked & chopped
2½ oz brisket, smoked & chopped
2½ oz pork, pulled or rib scrap
2 bay leaves
2½ cups crushed tomatoes
1 qt water
1½ oz cider vinegar

Instructions

Place beans into a large container and cover the beans with cold water (about 2:1 ratio of water to beans), then soak overnight. (Do not cover container). Place onions, garlic, and celery in a stock pot, and saute until softened. Add meats, cumin, paprika, pepper, salt, oregano, and Guajillo pepper. Drain the presoaked beans, then combine beans, 1 quart water, crushed tomatoes, and bay leaves. Combine the meat mixture and bean mixture in a large stock pot, and simmer at a low temperature and simmer until almost all the water is evaporated and beans are tender. When beans are cooked, season with vinegar to taste.

If too spicy, balance with a little brown sugar.

Navy beans soaked overnight are consistently soft compared to other types of beans.

COLLARD GREENS

This is a southern style item but it's also a pretty hardy green...in fact the OMC grows a little in its parking lot! Cooking them down with bacon fat makes them rich, but they're still a vegetable, so that makes them a nice break from all the meat involved in barbecuing. Go ahead and buy frozen collard greens if that's easier, it's a long slow kind of dish and we don't judge. Jalapeño Business makes for a delicious finishing touch.

Yield: 10 Servings

Ingredients

3 strips bacon (don't overcook)
2 cups yellow onion (diced)
1 Tbsp garlic (diced)
1/4 cup sugar
1½ cups water

1/4 cup bacon fat
4½ lbs collards (thawed if frozen)
1 Tbsp salt
1/2 tsp black pepper
1/3 cup apple cider vinegar

Instructions

Sauté bacon and remove from pan. Add diced onion and saute until deep golden brown. Add garlic and saute until fragrant. Add sugar to pan to melt. De-glaze pan with water, then add cider vinegar, salt, pepper and bacon fat. Stir until bacon fat is melted. Add collards. Cook until greens are tender, stirring frequently. Crumble bacon and add back in. Season to taste.

CLASSIC COLESLAW

Coleslaw is very popular in the Carolinas as a sandwich ingredient. The vinegar in this coleslaw helps cut the fat of a brisket, and the mayo cools the spicy taste of a pork rub. Depending on the time of year and where the OMC sources its cabbage, it evolves to be more or less spicy, so you could almost say it has "terroir"!

Yield:
4 Cups

Ingredients

Dressing
1/2 cup mayo
3 Tbsp cider vinegar
1½ Tbsp sugar
3/4 tsp salt
1/2 tsp black pepper
1/2 tsp celery seed

Slaw
1/4 lb shredded carrot
1 lb green cabbage
    (after being cut and cored)

Instructions

Cut cabbage in half and remove the core and set aside. Cut the ends of the carrots and set aside. Slice cabbage into 1/8" pieces (the thinner the better). In a large mixing bowl combine cabbage and shredded carrots. In separate bowl combine dressing ingredients and whisk to combine. Add the dressing to the veggie mix and mix until fully incorporated.

ELOTES TOPPING

Like the friend of a friend who "just needs to crash on your couch for the night", sometimes a summer special stays way longer than you expect it to. Louis learned about *elotes*—a Mexican-style grilled street food—on a trip to Mexico City and figured the "grilled" corn was close enough to "barbecued" corn to justify putting them on the menu. Everyone loved them and they stuck around.

Yield:
4 Cups

Serve with grilled corn. This recipe makes a *lot*— enough for 12 cups of corn if you serve it with 3 cups of corn kernels per cup of sauce. Or 12 cobs if you grill it and slather the sauce on, 1/3 cup per cob.

Ingredients

6 Tbsp jalapeño (minced)
2 garlic cloves (minced)
1 cup cilantro (fine chopped)
2 tsp chili powder
1 cup fresh lime juice
Zest from one lime

8 oz crumbled cojita cheese
1¼ cup mayo
3/4 cup & 2 Tbsp sour cream
1¾ tsp black pepper
1½ tsp sea salt

Note the grilled corn

Instructions

Combine all ingredients in a large container and mix well. Smear on whole grilled corn or mix with hot corn kernels. Leftover sauce? Store in the fridge.

CHEESY JALAPEÑO GRITS

A lot of us up north have tried runny and tasteless instant grits. When Louis was in Waco, Texas, he had grits served for breakfast. They were fluffy and filling, a totally new experience. A cook there told him good grits are boiled with water first to let the salt penetrate them. Only then do you add milk and butter. This was a dish so good Louis knew he wanted everyone to try it.

Yield: 1 Quart

Ingredients

3/4 cup 2% milk
1½ cup water
1 cup coarse yellow cornmeal
1 tsp salt
1/4 tsp black pepper
1 Tbsp butter
1/2 jalapeño, seeded & minced
3 oz shredded cheddar
2 oz shredded Gouda
1 Tbsp sour cream

Instructions

Combine water, salt, pepper, and jalapeño in pot and bring to a gentle boil. Slowly add corn meal while whisking to avoid lumps. Cook for 10 minutes. Add milk and whisk thoroughly. Turn heat to low and let simmer. Add butter. Let simmer until butter melts completely. Hardly any stirring is needed. After butter is melted, fold in all cheese and sour cream. Turn off heat and let sit for 10 minutes.

Best when made the day before than fresh from the pot. You may need to add water to adjust the consistency.

Grits: It's what's for dinner.

What's more Southern than a sweet potato bake? This is a fun dish because even though it's kind of a vegetable, it's also kind of a dessert. This is everything you'd want in French toast—eggs, sugar, vanilla, milk, cinnamon—but with a lot more butter. With a crispy brown sugar pecan topping, this is…okay, it's not even really a vegetable. It's just a dessert after all.

Yield: 3 Quarts

The Bake
Ingredients

3 lbs sweet potatoes, peeled and cubed
3/4 cup cane sugar
3 eggs
1 Tbsp vanilla

3/4 cup 2% milk
3/4 tsp cinnamon
1½ tsp salt
1/3 cup butter

The Topping
Ingredients

1 cup brown sugar
1/2 cup flour

1/3 cup softened butter
1 cup chopped pecans

Bake Instructions

Boil sweet potatoes, drain when tender. Mix sugar, eggs, vanilla, butter, milk, cinnamon and salt in mixer and beat until combined. Add mixture to drained sweet potatoes in a blender or food processor. Puree mixture until smooth, then place puree into a baking dish and bake uncovered at 350° for 25 minutes. Make topping while you bake. At 25 minutes, put topping on and bake another 5 minutes.

Topping Instructions

In a mixing bowl, toss flour and pecans. Add brown sugar and mix. Mix in butter, but do not overmix—form a crumble topping.

Julia Child once said "With enough butter, anything is good." This dish has plenty of it.

BACON AND BLUE CHEESE POTATO SALAD

Sister restaurant Duluth Grill did a bacon blue cheese coleslaw. Louis visited a number of barbecue places and felt the side dishes were sometimes lacking creativity. While the meat is always the priority at the OMC, they didn't want side dishes to be lame either. Enter this potato salad. With white balsamic, bacon, and blue cheese, it might not be "lean" but it's definitely not forgettable.

Yield: 1 Quart

Ingredients

2½ pounds baby red potatoes
1½ cups mayonnaise
1/2 red onion, diced
1/2 cup chopped parsley
1/4 cup white balsamic vinegar
1 Tbsp sugar
1 Tbsp French's mustard

1 Tbsp salt
1/2 Tbsp black pepper
1/3 cup bacon fat
3 slices chopped, cooked bacon
5 oz blue cheese crumbles

Instructions

Peel and cut potatoes into quarters. Steam or parboil baby red potatoes until cooked.

For the dressing, mix every ingredient except potatoes in a separate bowl. Don't mix too much—dressing should still be CHUNKY with onion and bacon clearly visible. Once potatoes are cooked, drain, allow to cool slightly, and mix in dressing while still a bit warm. Place in large container and put in the refrigerator to cool.

Sprinkle with chopped parsley when ready to serve

Bacon & Blue Cheese Potato Salad

PEAS AND PANCETTA

I (Robert) didn't realize I liked peas until I tried this. Peas and pancetta is an upgrade on peas with butter. Rendered pork fat makes it rich and the bites of pancetta give it a welcome chewiness.

**Yield:
2 Cups**

Ingredients
2 cups peas
¼ lb diced pancetta
Shaved Parmesan

Instructions
Saute and render the pancetta. Saute the peas in its fat until done (add some olive oil or butter if you need more fat). Top with Parmesan.

Substitute bacon for pancetta any time

Pricey Parmesan from the deli or discount from the dairy case? Buy the good stuff — better parm, better flavor.

Frozen peas are excellent for this dish

JALAPEÑO LIME SLAW

This can be enjoyed on its own, but it's meant to be an accompaniment to a sandwich. Jalapeño lime slaw adds welcome acidity to balance the heat of a pork belly sandwich or the Zip-A-Dee-Do-Dah.

Yield:
2 Cups

Ingredients

Vegetable Mix
1 lb green cabbage, shredded
1 small carrot, shredded
1/2 cup chopped cilantro
2½ Tbsp jalapeño (seeded, minced)

Dressing
1/2 cup olive oil
1/3 cup lime juice
4 tsp ground cumin
1 tsp salt
1/2 tsp black pepper

Instructions

In a large bowl, combine cabbage, carrots, cilantro and jalapeño. Combine dressing ingredients into blender and mix until combined. Stir into vegetable mix until lightly coated.

HAYSTACK ONIONS

Mmmm....fried onions. They're crunchy, and they go well with everything!

Ingredients
One onion
1/2 cup chicken dredge (page 77)

Instructions
Thinly slice onion. Toss them in chicken dredge. Shake excess dredge off. Fry until crispy, err on the side of lighter rather than darker.

Crunchy fried onions go on most things. Can you imagine green bean casserole with these little guys???

For a dish that can be described as "potatoes fried in oil", French fries are surprisingly technical. First you soak them to pull out starch so they don't stick together or become discolored. Then you want to pat them dry, otherwise your oil will scatter all over. It's good to par-fry them, then let cool, then fry again for maximum crispness.

Ingredients:
1 lb potatoes
enough oil for a deep fryer
Salt

You can use animal fat. We take beef trimmings from brisket, grind and slowly render them on the stovetop on low heat for a few hours until the fat chunks turn to liquid. Then we strain the hot fat and let it cool. You can use other animal fats like lard or duck fat too.

Directions:
Hand cut potatoes to the desired thickness, then soak in water overnight with a teaspoon of salt. This helps remove the excess starch so they fry better and don't stick together. Strain and pat dry before frying.

If you want them extra crispy, par-fry them. That means you blanch them in 380° oil for a few moments. Don't crisp them at all, leave them opaque. Remove them from the oil, drain them and then re-fry until golden brown. That will make for a crispier fry. Salt and serve with Malt Vinegar Aioli (page 15).

Add water to sliced potatoes...

...and add salt and soak overnight

Malt Vinegar Aioli (page 15)

Bacon has had quite the journey over the last 20 years—it went from Dietary Enemy Number One to trendy ingredient, and now it's yesterday's news. But it never really stopped tasting good. This sweet, tangy salsa gets a hint of smokiness from the bacon. Or, if you want to omit it, just make a vegan corn relish! We try and be flexible with our recipes, so you should as well.

Yield: 4 Cups

Ingredients:

Relish
2 pieces cooked bacon, chopped
2 cups frozen corn
1/4 cup red pepper (small dice)
2 Tbsp + 1 tsp jalapeños (small dice)

Brine
1/2 cup red onion (small dice)
5 fl oz cider vinegar
5 fl oz water
2 Tbsp sugar
3/4 tsp mustard seed
1½ tsp salt
1/3 tsp fennel seed

Directions:

Combine all brine ingredients in a small stock pot and bring to a boil. Meanwhile, combine all relish ingredients into storage container. Once brine comes to a boil, pour over corn mix, cover and refrigerate.

PICKLES

Y ou can always go buy pickled jalapeños or onions if you want. You don't have to make them. It's fun to make them—and we think it's worth it—but a jar of jalapeños is pretty easy. But there's a reason you're looking at these recipes, and it's probably because you're a true pickle aficionado. You should know that just the right blend of spices takes you from "what you get at the store" to "heaven in a jar". And if that's what you want, you've come to the right place.

BRINED ONIONS

Onions are a curious food. When raw, they're hot! When fried, they're mild and savory. Pickling onions gets you to a sort of middle ground, where the heat is tempered but still present. Make these ahead of time, as they'll keep for a couple of months in the brine if you don't accidentally add contaminants (use a clean fork). Like both our pickle recipes, these are refrigerator pickles, so in spite of the Kerr® Mason® jar used on the next page, neither pressure cooker nor canning knowledge is required.

Yield: 1 Quart

Ingredients:
1 lb red onion (julienne)

Brine
1¾ cup cider vinegar
3/4 cup sugar
3/4 Tbsp mustard seeds
3/4 Tbsp salt
1 tsp celery seed
3/4 tsp ground ginger

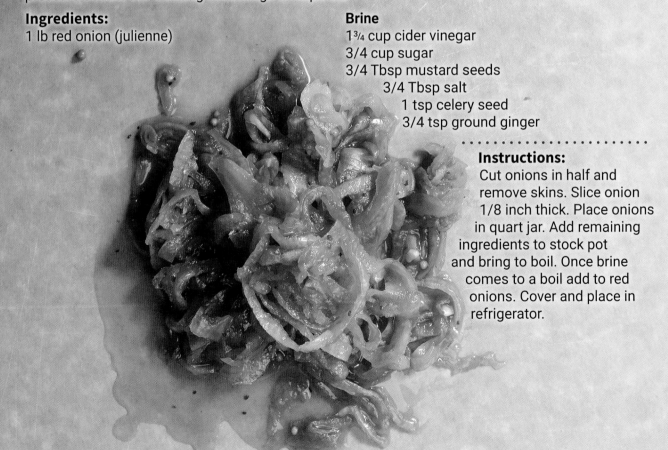

Instructions:
Cut onions in half and remove skins. Slice onion 1/8 inch thick. Place onions in quart jar. Add remaining ingredients to stock pot and bring to boil. Once brine comes to a boil add to red onions. Cover and place in refrigerator.

Pickling jalapeños cuts down their heat, but it doesn't remove it entirely. The Scoville rating on a jalapeño ranges from 2,500 to 10,000 Scoville Units, so you are always taking a risk when you pop them on your food! If you really find your face on fire, don't drink milk—bite a lemon! The acid helps cool you down faster than almost anything.

Yield: 1.5 Quarts

A little bit sweeter, these are closer to a bread-and-butter pickle than the straight vinegar flavor you might get with jalapeños on nachos at a ballpark. Like our previous pickle recipe, these are refrigerator pickles so no canning knowledge is required.

Ingredients:
1 pound (about 20 large) sliced jalapeños

Brine
3 cups cider vinegar
1 cup sugar
1 Tbsp yellow mustard seeds
1 Tbsp salt
1½ tsp celery seed
1½ tsp turmeric
1 tsp ground ginger

Instructions:
Place ingredients for the brine in a large sauce pan. Bring to a boil and then let simmer for 5 minutes. Remove stems from the peppers and slice 1/8-inch thick. Place pepper into a clean quart jar and pour in brine while it is hot. Screw on the cover and refrigerate. Let sit at least a week before enjoying.

"We'll Never Open A Restaurant Ever Again"

HOW THE OMC STARTED

When you lose money—especially a lot of money, especially at a young age—it has a way of changing you. So when Tom and Jaima Hanson, Hotshot Young Restaurant Owners, decided to open Bayfront Grill in Superior, and decided to open it in a defunct hotel kitchen, and decided to open it just one year after they took over The Duluth Grill. Well, it changed them. In fact, it almost bankrupt them.

"Phone's for you, Tom," Jaima said sweetly in the middle of a 12 hour shift. In front of customers, they always used the code. Tom smiled and put down the plate. He knew who was calling. He went to the back office.

"We have no money," he explained, for the third time that day to the third vendor of the day or maybe the eighth of the week. It all ran together. "This call is actually taking me away from earning money to pay you with."

The same people kept calling.

The OMC building in 2016, well before there was a "Craft District."

"If you don't believe me, please take me to court," Tom explained, "Then we can both agree that I don't have the money. But we will pay you."

The vendors grumbled. But between a chance at *something* and guaranteed *nothing*, they picked the *something*. The lesser of two evils, maybe, but easier than a lawsuit—and Minnesotans don't really go in big for lawsuits.

Something happened. Tom and Jaima paid back every penny, over six grinding years.

"We'll never open a restaurant ever again," Tom promised.

But time passed, and the old legends were forgotten. The Duluth Grill prospered. Soon a new generation rose, who did not know the old ways. Louis, the son and heir, began to wax powerful in management. His best friend and "adopted Hanson" Jeff rose to the upper ranks as well. Dan, back of the house, became the head chef.

"When I looked at Jeff and Louis and Dan, I realized they were going to want more responsibility," Tom says. "I thought if I didn't have something else for them to do I could lose one, two or all three of them."

And so, two heartbroken entrepreneurs 'learned to love again'. Naturally, they wanted to take it slow. When a building in the undeveloped Lincoln Park neighborhood came up for sale for $90,000 in 2013, they were hesitant to jump in.

"That summer I went in for a physical. A month or two later I was having my thyroid taken out for thyroid cancer," Tom recalls. "I thought 'If I have health issues, the last thing I want to do is start a second location.' So we backed out."

> *"How low can you go? Whatever you can send an offer for with a straight face," the attorney responded.*

Tom, Jeff and Louis, at the beginning of the OMC building's restoration.

A year later, though, that building was $57,000. And Tom started asking his attorney the number one question of every limbo contest: how low can you go?

"Whatever you can send an offer for with a straight face," the attorney responded.

"I sent him an offer for $30,000 as-is with no inspection," Tom says. "They sent me a counteroffer for $47,000. I made a final offer at $37,000. Ten minutes later they accepted it. At that time I thought 'I just did the dumbest thing in my life'."

But at the closing, it turned out Tom was accidentally a very savvy negotiator.

"They handed me *two* property tax statements," he says. "We thought we were just buying a building, but we had bought a full sized lot as well. For $37,000 we had bought 75 feet on Duluth's defining street."

The OMC building under construction

Our story has now taken us to 2015. To appreciate just how odd it is that the OMC exists at all, you have to understand the vision Tom and Jaima brought to their new place.

At this point, The Duluth Grill had been lauded for its local, organic, often vegetarian food. The Hansons were fascinated with their carbon footprint and the health benefits of veganism, juicing, and raw food. They went to California for a four-week "uncooking" class, where they learned to use dehydrators and blenders to create fresh and nutritious vegan food.

Aka: not pork rinds.

And yet.

"If there was anyone in the world that should do well in raw vegan food, it should be California," Jaima says. "And they struggled with it. That exposed us to the reality. Meat and protein is in our DNA."

Gone were the linen tablecloths, candles, a quiet date night experience. Gone was the cheap kitchen with no hood or oven. But Louis, who had just returned from a trip out west, had two ideas. He thought the new place should either focus on biscuits and gravy or straight-up barbecue. He convinced his parents that southern cooking was on the upswing and it was time to get in on it. With the Duluth Grill already occupying the breakfast niche and barbecue allowing for more options, the team discussed going from "No Meat" to "All Meat". But the decision became a lot firmer after an off-the-cuff interview.

"While we were remodeling in 2015, a lady walked in with a clipboard and a piece of paper," Tom says. "I thought she was an inspector, but it turned out she was from the Duluth News-Tribune. I told her 'we're thinking of doing barbecue'. Public response was overwhelming."

The remodel took hundreds of hours, and the OMC gang did much of the work themselves.

Now the group had only two obstacles left.

1. Remodel an enormous building

2. Master an entirely new cuisine

Step 1 was brute force. The electricity went off and the crowbars came out. Over 1,000 man hours, the Duluth Grill gang smashed, hammered, and Sawzalled its way to glory before contractors came in.

"Trying to redo a 130 year old building wasn't going to be a home handyman job," Tom says.

Step 2 would require a little more finesse. How could a pack of clueless northerners learn the secrets of southern barbecue?

"The more you know, the more you realize you don't know about it," OMC partner Jeff Petcoff says. "Trying to do it justice was the biggest thing for us."

The way they started figuring out barbecue is another story entirely...and we'll cover it on page 43. OMC

APPETIZERS

These appetizers serve two functions. On the one hand, they get the party started. On the other, they keep it going the next day by giving you a venue to showcase leftover sauces and meats. When you barbecue, you generally smoke a lot of meat at once. So keep it in the fridge or freezer and chop off chunks for these recipes. By the way, feel free to mix and match. Brisket and pulled pork make great quesadillas. Throw some smoked chicken on your nachos instead of pork. It's your party...Swap the sauce if you want to.

Pork Belly
Lettuce Wraps

An OMC fan favorite. Frying tortilla chips in-house makes them a little thicker, and topping them with cheese sauce, pulled pork, Chipotle Cilantro Sauce, and jalapeño makes them dinner before you eat dinner.

Yield:
4 servings of nachos

Ingredients
1 large bag tortilla chips
6 oz Cheese Sauce (page 17)
3 oz pico de gallo
2 oz pickled jalapeños (page 32 or use store-bought)
5 oz pulled pork
2 oz sour cream
2 oz Chipotle Cilantro Sauce (page 11)
1 oz green onion
Cilantro (optional)

Instructions
Combining cold ingredients with hot cheese leads to lukewarm nachos. So gently warm your pulled pork until it's just over room temperature (don't overcook it). Leave pico, jalapeños, Chipotle Cilantro Sauce, and sour cream out on the counter for 20 minutes just to take the edge off the refrigerator chill. Get your cheese sauce blistering hot, then assemble the dish quickly. Top with green onion and cilantro, and drizzle with sour cream. Crisis averted.

Cilantro. Totally optional... but totally recommended.

SMOKED CHICKEN QUESADILLA

Simple is beautiful. If you have smoked chicken and cheese, throw that in. If you have homemade pico on the side, throw that in there too and top with sour cream. You want to make this even simpler at home? Roll the tortilla up and melt the cheese in the microwave. No griddle necessary!

Yield: 1 Quesadilla

Ingredients

12 inch tortilla
4 oz shredded cheddar
2 oz pico de gallo
5oz pulled chicken
1 piece of Bibb lettuce with additional 1 oz pico as garnish

1 oz Chipotle Cilantro Sauce (page 11)
1 oz sour cream
2 oz cheddar
1 oz chopped green onion

Instructions

Put cheddar, 2 oz pico, and chicken in the tortilla and fold in half. Put on skillet on medium heat until cheese is melted (flip halfway through). Top with lettuce, additional pico, Chipotle Cilantro Sauce, sour cream, cheddar, and green onion. Garnish with extra pico on lettuce.

A Texas Twinkie is a cream-cheese stuffed bacon-wrapped jalapeño. A Minnesota Twinkie is just a regular Twinkie, so this dish needed another name. Enter the Jalapeño Brisket Bomb. Jalapeños range a lot in spiciness, and the smoking process takes some—but not all—of the heat out. Will you burn your mouth and cry? Will it be mild? It's all luck of the draw.

**Yield:
10 Bombs**

Ingredients
8 oz cream cheese
3 strips cooked bacon, chopped
1 Tbsp + 1 tsp pork rub (page 6)
1/4 cup + 2 Tbsp chopped green onion
3/4 cup minced brisket
5 jalapeños
Optional: extra sauce for drizzling
    on top (you pick)

Instructions
Add cream cheese, bacon, pork rub, green onions, and chopped brisket into a mixer and mix well. Cut jalapeños in half and de-seed. Leave tops of jalapeños intact. Fill jalapeño halves with cream cheese mixture. Smoke jalapeños for 20 minutes at 230º. Drizzle sauce on top.

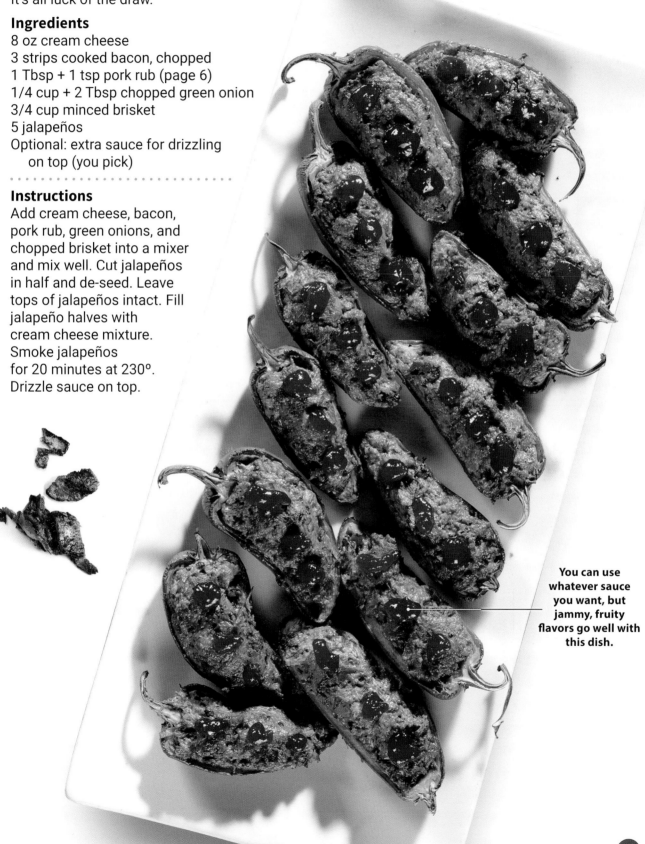

You can use whatever sauce you want, but jammy, fruity flavors go well with this dish.

PORK BELLY LETTUCE WRAPS

Pork belly isn't light. But this is as light as it gets. Quick, spicy-sweet, and perfect for summertime. Bibb lettuce, crunchy cabbage, slaw, a little maple syrup and boom! An appetizer worth drooling over. Vegetarians in the party? Substitute black beans.

Yield: 12 Wraps

Ingredients
24 pieces of Bibb lettuce
1 cup corn relish (page 30)
1 cup jalapeño lime slaw
    (page 28)
12 pieces of pork belly (page
    55) glazed with Korean BBQ
    sauce (page 12)
Drizzle of maple syrup

Instructions
Assemble each lettuce wrap with a couple pieces of lettuce, a chunk of pork belly, and a bit of relish and slaw. Then drizzle with maple syrup.

Bibb
Lettuce

Pork
Belly

Crunchy
Cabbage

Pure
Maple
Syrup

Korean
BBQ Sauce

Pimento cheese is a classic southern dish with cream cheese, cheddar, and pimento peppers. The OMC adds a northern twist with its smoked salmon. This is a salmon-cheese spread with a little bit of a kick.

**Yield:
2 Cups**

Ingredients
1 cup shredded cheddar
   cheese
4 oz softened cream cheese
1/4 cup mayo
2 Tbsp roasted red pepper
   (diced small)
1/4 Tbsp Nashville Hot
   Chicken Rub (page 7)
1/2 lb smoked salmon, flaked
   (page 90 or use store-bought)

Instructions
Add all ingredients except salmon to bowl and mix well. Fold salmon into mixture (preserving the "flakes" of salmon meat).

Smoked
Salmon

Brined
Onion

Salmon
Pimento Dip

Thousands of Miles, Tens of Thousands of Calories, and One Cramped Car

AN EPIC SERIES OF BARBECUE ROADTRIPS
−Or− *How The OMC Gang Went "Down South"*
Retrieved The Secrets Of Barbecue
& Changed Their Corner of the World Forever

There is a hum every road makes as it zooms under you. Some rumble: *thwackathwackathwacka*. Some buzz. Some almost purr. A road trip, where the hours turn into days and the days turn into weeks, has a beauty all its own. The swollen red sun, the deep purple sky, the crystal stars — and Nebraska (we won't talk about that.)

But mind-numbingly boring scenery aside, the Hansons don't regret putting in thousands of miles on the open road. Our cast starts with Tom and Jaima, born Minnesotans who grew up eating Swedish meatballs. There was their son Louis, who had never smoked a brisket. Rounding out the crew were honorary Hanson Jeff Petcoff and chef Dan LeFebvre. Both men were very good at meatloaf...not so much at smoked pork.

In short, they were not a barbecue dream team. But by 2015, they had committed to opening a huge restaurant dedicated to a cuisine they knew nothing about.

"We were spending $1.2 million to open this place all-in," OMC founder Tom Hanson says. "We thought 'if we're going to do BBQ, we'd better learn BBQ'."

So they hatched a plan. Over a series of trips, they'd immerse themselves in the BBQ culture of the Deep South. They traveled from region to region, learning its ways and volunteering in famous kitchens. But first, they had to get out of the bathroom.

This scene takes place when Jeff, Dan, and Louis were eating some barbecue in Waco, Texas. Dan had gone into the bathroom stall—as one does—when he heard voices. *Female* voices.

"A steady stream of women came into the bathroom for some time," Jeff recalls. "We were just sitting at the table wondering 'what is taking him so long?'"

Dan eventually escaped the women's rest room. But the life of barbecue had gotten its clutches on all of them. Louis and Tom spent a week working at two different restaurants in Kansas City. Tom and Jaima took a motorhome to Tennessee, Louisiana, South Carolina, and Kentucky. Once—because barbecue does strange things to your head—they drove six hours just to get to a restaurant in North Carolina. Louis, his wife Ashley, and their kids took a family trip to Austin Texas with grandma and grandpa,

Dan catching shutteye in the motorhome

then met barbecue legend Joe Slack in Waco on the way home. From Nashville to NOLA, from Austin to St. Louis, they criss-crossed BBQ Country. There were a few close calls.

"I remember going through a stretch in the middle of the night getting down to an empty tank," Jeff recalls. "There weren't any gas stations for quite some time. We took the old RV to its max."

The eating part was more fun, but also required a certain amount of endurance. During the 150 or so meals they ate on the road (!), the only option was sharing.

"We order a lot and we will share it with the person next to us," Jaima says. "People are like "whaaat?!" It's a lot of food we order–you've got to experience everything."

Even while sharing plates with random strangers, it ended up being a lot to swallow.

"Some of the trips we felt just disgusting when we came home," Tom says. "Eating is not fun when you do it as part of research. I don't think people understand that."

Barbecue inspires a certain amount of passion, and popular restaurants often see long lines and big crowds. But just like with bands or sports teams, those who travel the furthest are often the most dedicated supporters. On their barbecue pilgrimage, the Hansons were able to get the best seats in the house. Sometimes.

"One time we were [at Pappy's] in St Louis, and Tom and I got there really early in the morning," Jaima says. "We pulled our motorhome outside and made some coffee. We were super excited because we wanted to be the first people there. I think they opened up at 11, but there were no cars." By 10, even by 10:30, there were still no cars. That's when the doubts started.

"We went around the back and there were 100 people there," Jaima says. "Apparently you go in through the back and not the front."

Another fond memory of waiting in line was Franklin BBQ in Austin TX. "The line there starts at 8 in the morning and by 11 there are 100 or 200 people in line," Tom says. "People are sharing their beer and coffee with the people next to them. It's kind of like we're all tailgating to go to a restaurant. It's like when you're a kid and you go to a really loud Baptist church with your friend where people are singing and talking and super friendly. You're like, 'wow, this is not what I'm used to, but it's kind of fun.' It sucks you in."

But the real magic happened in the back of the house. At Q39 in Kansas City, the staff showed Tom and the gang around the kitchen. Todd Johns, who owns Plowboys in Kansas City, went a step further, and let the team work with him.

"We go in and have a Minnesota work ethic," Tom says. "We're willing to clean, work as soon as we're set up, work quickly until we're done. I think they were surprised."

Franklin BBQ in Austin TX
In barbecue, even waiting in line is a party. Think of tailgating, but instead of a ending with a football game, you end up eating a brisket instead.

Photo by:
Larry D. Moore
CC BY-SA 4.0.

There were a couple more stints—a restaurant in Austin, another in Kansas City. But maybe the biggest win was Waco, where Tom met barbecue pro Joe Slack of Red Wagon BBQ. Not formally, no. But by wandering into a closed area.

"We're not open Thursdays," Joe recalls. "But I was at the pit, and Tom just came walking up."

They got to talking about Tom's travels so far, and Joe asked Tom what his favorite place had been. Tom said it was Franklin Barbecue in Austin, Texas.

"Well, that's pretty interesting," Joe said. "Because those are the ones I learned from."

The story there is personal, as many in the barbecue world seem to be. Joe teaches guitar making classes and one of his students had a son working the pit at Franklin Barbecue. When Joe wanted to get into the business, his student's son John Lewis Jr taught him.

Dan, Joe Slack, Louis and Jeff after completing Joe's *How To Cook Brisket for Beginners* class.

Joe said he'd be happy to teach anyone Tom wanted to send. So Jeff, Louis, and Dan went down to Waco and spent a few days learning at Red Wagon.

"It was just fun," Joe recalls. "What's really amazing about it is that I've only been cooking barbecue for a few years. And here these guys are experienced chefs, but I was able to help them do something they wanted to do."

But at the end of 8,000 miles, the OMC had found what it was looking for. Drop by and you'll probably hear a few more tales of the trips.

"99% of the people in BBQ are willing to show you how they cook it," Tom says. "It's really like a big friendly community, and there's a huge sense of pride." OMC

OINK

This is the core of the menu at any barbecue restaurant. And your key word here is *practice*. Pay attention to the meat. Take notes on what you did (cook time, temperature, wood used, anything that stood out or seemed off). Keep getting better! We have some tips for you on buying a smoker and finding wood elsewhere in this book, but mainly at this point you just have to get in there and start experimenting. We wish you luck.

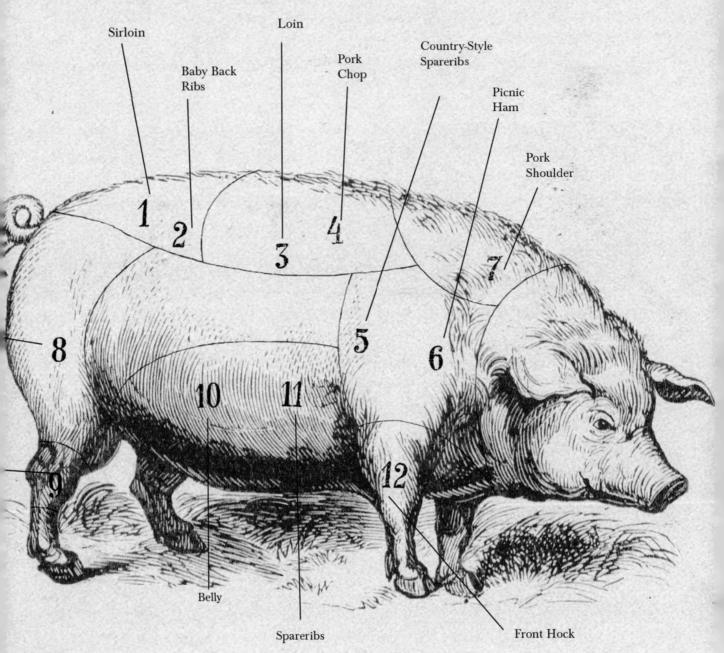

Sirloin

Loin

Baby Back Ribs

Pork Chop

Country-Style Spareribs

Picnic Ham

Pork Shoulder

1 2 3 4 5 6 7

8

9

10 11 12

Belly

Spareribs

Front Hock

HOW TO COOK PORK
(Pork Butt, Ribs, Pulled Pork, and Pork Belly)

PORK BUTT

Time Commitment: 2 or 3 days

Easy Way Out: Pre-cooked pork shoulder from the grocery store or a crock pot recipe. (This won't fool anyone on its own, but it will get the job done in composed dishes or sandwiches).

Pork butt actually refers to pork shoulder. The name comes from butts, the barrels used to store pork around the time of the Revolutionary War. In fact, that's why you'll sometimes see pork shoulders called "Boston butts"— it was considered a specialty of New England. If you're wondering what meat you get from the pig's upper thigh and *gluteus maximus* (what you might call its butt), it's ham!

So "pork butt", or more accurately shoulder, is a moderately tough cut with a good amount of connective tissue. It responds really well to low and slow cooking, which is why Minnesotans slap it in a crock pot and southerners put it in the grill.

Ingredients	In The Smoker*	In The Pan
1 pork butt (about 8 pounds)	1 log sugar maple	(Later in the recipe,
1 cup pork rub (page 6)	1 log oak	please read ahead)
	Water as needed	8 cups water
	(depends on your smoker)	1 cup cider vinegar

Instructions follow

* **Read more about smokers on page 113**

Pork Butt Instructions

Typical Pork butt, approx. 8 lbs.

Score pork butt in criss-cross pattern. Get down below the fat and just into the meat itself...

...you may be cutting an inch deep..

Rub pork butt *generously* with Pork rub (see page 6). Be sure to penetrate all the cuts.

Back side of pork

Flip the butt and rub back and sides as well.

This is how the butt should look after the 2-3 day refrigeration

Place pork butt on a sheet pan with large bag over pan and place into the fridge to sit for 2–3 days.

Pre-heat the smoker to 230°. Add water to the bottom of the smoker, and 1 log of oak and 1 log of sugar maple fire wood.

Remember to periodically monitor the temp!

Place pork butt in smoker. Smoke pork butt for 6–8 hours or until the pork reaches 170°. (Check every two hours to ensure constant temp).

Remove pork from smoker.

Place pork butt in deep pan: add 8 cups of water and 1/2 cup of apple cider vinegar.

Ensure that pork butt is fork tender all the way through.

Place in 350° oven until the internal temp reaches 203°.

If you're going to make pulled pork (see following page), don't throw away the liquid.

Remove from oven and serve.

Time Commitment: A few hours if you already have the pork butt smoked

Easy Way Out: Grab the slow cooker and pull up a recipe online or buy premade. It won't be smoky, but it will do. Just make sure to get the un-sauced version so you can customize!

Pulled pork! So simple, but so delicious. Many of our sandwich and composed recipes use this versatile ingredient. Throw it in tacos, season it to taste, even use it to amp up a salad.

Ingredients
5 lbs smoked pork butt, 1/4 cup pork rub (page 6) and 1/2 cup cider vinegar

Pulled Pork Instructions

If you kept your smoked pork with the liquid, remove the smoked and fully cooked meat from the fridge, skim the fat off of top of the liquid, and save the pork stock to add back to the pulled pork.

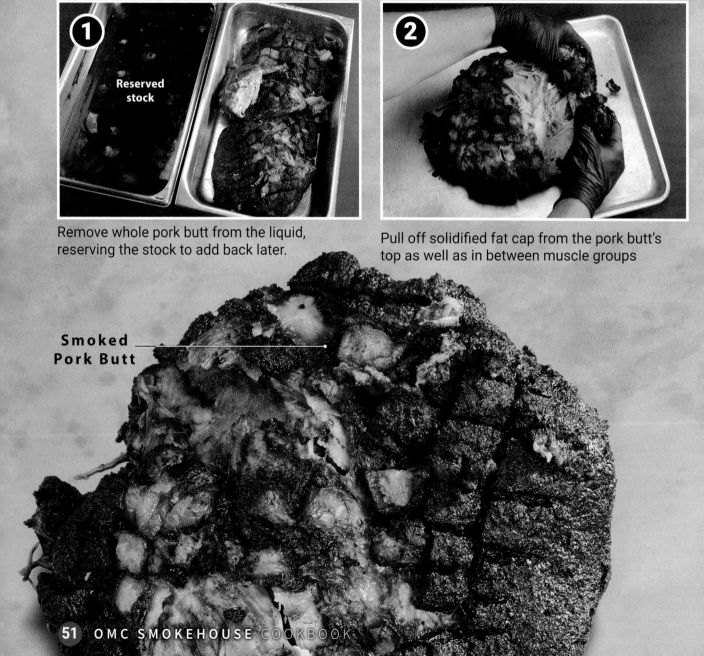

1. Reserved stock

Remove whole pork butt from the liquid, reserving the stock to add back later.

2.

Pull off solidified fat cap from the pork butt's top as well as in between muscle groups

Smoked Pork Butt

Once pork fat is removed, pull the pork butt apart in large chunks.

Weigh out the amount of meat and adjust recipe accordingly. (You may need to scale rub and vinegar up or down)

Mix in pork rub.

Gently mix in cider vinegar, and any remaining pork stock. Do not over-mix pulled pork or it will lose its texture.

Place pulled pork into an oven or pot and reheat until the pork reaches a temperature of 165°.

Time Commitment: A few hours

Easy Way Out: Grab a simple oven-bake recipe online. Make a dynamite BBQ sauce and they'll still taste pretty good. DO NOT BOIL.

Ribs should be tender but have a bit of chew. If they're falling off the bone so much that they melt in your mouth, you have taken a drastic wrong turn! This is one reason boiling ribs is such a no-no. They need drier heat and smoke. Note that while it's kind of a pain the first few times you try it, it is VERY important to remove the silverskin, a thin membrane on the back side of the ribs. If you leave the skin membrane on, it will block absorption of smoke and stop the rub from working its way in.

Ingredients
1 rack St. Louis style ribs
Heavily rub (up to a cup) Pork rub (page 6)

Smoker
1 log sugar maple firewood
1 log oak firewood
Water as needed (depends on your smoker)

St. Louis Style Pork Rib Instructions

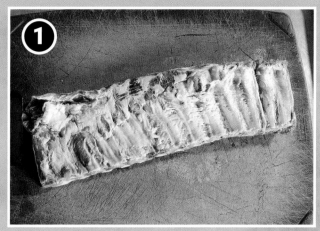

Is there a skin on the rib's underside? If so peel skin membrane from the back side of ribs using a paper towel.

Add 1 log of oak and 1 log of sugar maple (depending on the size of your smoker) along with water in the bottom of the smoker.

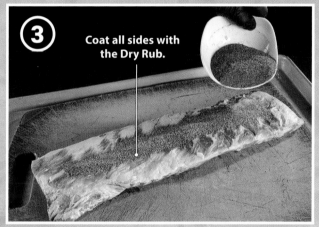

Coat all sides with the Dry Rub.

Rub ribs with Pork rub (see page 6) immediately before smoking.

Mist with cider vinegar every hour.

Place ribs in smoker at 230° for 2–4 hours. (If you're cooking more than one, load it bottom to top).

NOTE: Ribs should be tender but not falling off the bone.

When ribs are fully cooked, they should release slightly from the bone. Remove from smoker and let rest for 20 minutes before serving.

Time Commitment: Three or four days.

Easy Way Out: There really isn't one. If you fry some thick cut bacon and drizzle Korean BBQ glaze on it, you could make a halfway decent lettuce wrap, or even a BLT inspired by our pork belly sandwich. But It would not be *our* lettuce wrap or *our* pork belly sandwich.

Cured or uncured, fried or rendered, smoked or not: pork belly is an inspiration. International forms exist from German Speck to Italian pancetta to French lardons. Here in the US, we usually call it bacon! Korea and China have often used thicker cuts—we've borrowed that tradition for our pork belly. Cured, braised, and smoked it's a whole new twist on this humble meat. How did pork chops get so popular when pork belly was an option the whole time?

Ingredients

1 pork belly	1/2 cup coarse black pepper	Oil for frying	**Smoker**
2 lbs salt	3 cinnamon sticks	1 onion, sliced	1 log sugar maple firewood
24 oz brown sugar	2 Tbsp cayenne pepper	3 garlic cloves	1 log oak firewood
9 bay leaves	6 whole cloves	2 jalapeños, chopped	Water as needed
3/4 cup granulated garlic		12 oz can of stout beer	
		2 cups of water	

A. MAKING THE BELLY RUB

Combine everything in the first two ingredient columns except bay leaves and cloves.

Put bay leaves and cloves in a blender and blend into powder.

Mix with first mixture. Set aside two cups for later use.

You can use various sizes of pork belly

Coat sides of pork belly with cure. Refrigerate for two days before smoking.

B. SMOKING & FINISHING THE BELLY

Smoke cured bellies at 230° for 3 hours. Skin should start to peel easily. Smoke longer if needed.

Bellies should be smoked skin side down with fat on top (fat will then soak into the meat).

Once smoked, place bellies (skin up) in a large pan with onion, garlic, jalapeno, beer, and water.

Peel skin off completely.

Add extra belly rub and braise at 400° for 20 minutes or until caramelization happens.

If not tong tender, wrap & return to oven.

Check now for "tong tenderness". Push tongs into the belly: if they can penetrate the meat, the belly is done. Drain liquid.

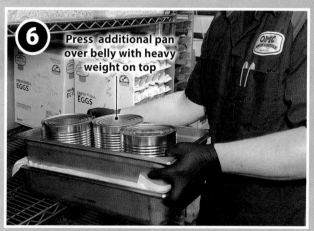

Press additional pan over belly with heavy weight on top

Press belly for one day to even out the cut. Slice, and either deep fry or saute in a pan just before eating.

This hearty dish is good in the wintertime when you want something to stick to your ribs. Build it up like a lasagna in a 9x13 pan and you'll be the most popular person at your next potluck. Don't be too rigid with the ingredients suggested here. We're going to studiously avoid the overused "go hog wild" joke (except I guess we sort of just made it anyway), but it's your party and you can ad-lib if you want to. Like cilantro? That might taste pretty good here. Have some extra BBQ sauce? Could be good. Switch out the protein for another meat, do it risotto style with a rice base, or use this same basic concept for an omelet or a sandwich. We're just trying to inspire you. Recipes are merely a starting point--be free and play around with new ideas!

Yield: 4-6 Servings

Ingredients
6 cups Cheesy Jalapeño Grits (page 24)
1/2 cup bacon corn relish (page 30)
1/2 cup brined onions (page 31 or use
    store-bought)
1/4 cup pickled jalapeños (page 32
    or use store-bought)
20 oz pulled pork
6 oz shredded cheddar
1/4 cup green onions

Instructions
Gently warm pulled pork in a pan, then mix grits, relish, onions, jalapeños, and pulled pork in a large cast iron pot. Top with cheddar. Melt under broiler. Top with ¼ cup green onions.

Nonstick pans or pans with plastic handles won't hold up under the heat of a broiler. So cast iron doesn't just look cool—it's practical as well!

The even easier version of the OMC tacos! This is the way to use an arbitrarily large number of OMC leftovers. Use elotes, sauce, meat, or whatever you have on hand! Or maybe we should say "whatever you have on hand, except for Toffee Bundt Cake". Once again, lining these up and letting everyone make their own is a fun way to serve this to a group.

Yield: 4-6 Servings

Ingredients

1⅓ cups uncooked rice
Juice of one lime
1/4 cup chopped cilantro plus more to taste
2 cups of corn
1½ cups cheese sauce (page 17)
2 cups OMC beans (page 22)
20 oz pulled pork
3/4 cup brined onions (page 31 or use store-bought)
1/4 cup pickled jalapeños (page 32 or use store-bought)
3/4 cup diced tomato
1/2 cup elotes dressing (page 23)
Drizzle chipotle cilantro sauce (page 11)
4 lime wedges
Tortilla chips to taste

Instructions

Cook rice. Stir in lime juice and 1/4 cup chopped cilantro. Sauté rice with corn until warm. Mix in cheese sauce, beans, pulled pork, onion, jalapeño, tomato, and elote dressing. Drizzle with chipotle BBQ to taste, top with lime wedges, remaining cilantro, and tortilla chips.

We said Minnesota doesn't have a barbecue culture, but that's not entirely true. Every grad party and most funerals and weddings have dinner rolls, slow cooker "BBQ" pork, and creamy side dishes. It turns out "bun, pork, coleslaw" is a popular sandwich in the Carolinas, so here you go—a gourmet version of what you'd eat with your youth hockey team in a Lutheran church basement.

Yield: 1 Sandwich

Ingredients
Brioche bun
2 pieces Bibb lettuce
2 oz Classic Coleslaw
(page 23)
5 oz pulled pork
2 oz haystack onions
(page 28)

Instructions
Toast bun. Put lettuce and coleslaw on it. Gently reheat pulled pork in a pan. Pop it on top. Top with haystack onions and the other half of the bun and eat up.

Why brioche buns? They have a nice, neutral flavor but stand up to a nice hearty sandwich (we like our sandwiches sloppy!)

KOREAN BBQ PORK BELLY SANDWICH

The pork belly is what makes this sandwich. It's cured for two days, smoked, braised, cooled, pressed, fried, and then glazed with Korean barbecue. Then it's offset with a bit of crunchy fresh cilantro lime slaw. People go nuts over it.

Yield: 1 Sandwich

Ingredients

Brioche bun
2 oz jalapeño lime
    slaw (page 28)
5 oz pork belly
    (page 55)
Korean barbecue sauce
    to taste (page 12)

Instructions

Toast brioche bun. If you haven't fried the pork belly yet, it's best to do right before eating. (If you have, reheat it). Glaze with Korean Barbecue Sauce. Put jalapeño lime slaw on first, follow with the pork belly and pickled jalapeños. This sandwich is fairly simple, but once you've cured, braised, smoked, fried, and glazed a piece of pork belly, you're probably not looking for any extra steps.

Jalapeño
lime slaw

Sandwiches should be fun. This starts with pulled pork, then gets zip from lime, "a dee" from pepper jack, and... "do da"...from...I'm drawing a total blank. Just eat it.

Yield: 1 Sandwich

Ingredients
Brioche bun
2 oz jalapeño lime
   slaw (page 28)
5 oz pulled pork
1 slice pepper jack
   cheese
1 oz pickled jalapeños
   (page 32)

Instructions
Take jalapeño lime slaw and pickled jalapeños out of the fridge half an hour before making the sandwiches to take the edge of the chill. Toast brioche bun. Gently reheat pulled pork in a pan. Top with cheese while pork is hot (maybe even while pork is still in the pan) to get it melty. Assemble with slaw and jalapeños. Now you have the perfect sandwich!

Brioche buns are a touch richer than the average bun and stand up well to hearty barbecue.

KOREAN BBQ PORK BELLY SOBA NOODLE BOWL

Why soba noodles at a barbecue place? Well, it does get hot in the summer...and sometimes you have one person at your table who just isn't feeling like a heavy dish. This is for that person. The sauce is umami rich and the cabbage and onions make it crunchy!

Yield:
1 Serving

Ingredients
4 oz uncooked soba noodles
Enough soba noodle dressing to coat noodles, about 1 Tbsp, or more to taste (page 16)
1/4 cup spicy boiled pecans (see below)
Lime wedge
1/2 cup peas
1/2 cup cabbage
1/4 cup brined onions
Chopped scallions and cilantro to taste
5 oz fried pork belly glazed in 1.5 oz Korean BBQ sauce

Instructions
Boil the noodles according to package directions. Rinse in cold water and drain. Toss them in dressing. Mix in pecans, peas, cabbage, onions or plate as seen in photo. Place pork belly on top. Top with scallions and cilantro, plate with lime.

Spicy boiled pecans (see below)

Pork Belly page 55

Green Peas

Soba Noodles

SPICY BOILED PECANS

Boil 2 cups pecans with water in a saute pan for 1 minute. In a mixing bowl, combine 1 Tbsp orange juice and 1 egg white. Add pecans. In a separate bowl, combine 2 Tbsp brown sugar, 1 tsp Nashville hot chicken rub, and 1 tsp salt. Add wet pecan mixture to bowl. Toss and spread out on a baking sheet. Bake at 350° until evenly cooked to a dry crunchy consistency.

MOO

That's a big cow, but the only section you need to worry about for barbecue is section 15. Right between the front two legs, the brisket is initially one of the toughest cuts of beef. But under low, slow heat, it becomes incredibly tender flavorful. Brisket is complex, and it's technical, but with practice and patience, you'll find your way.

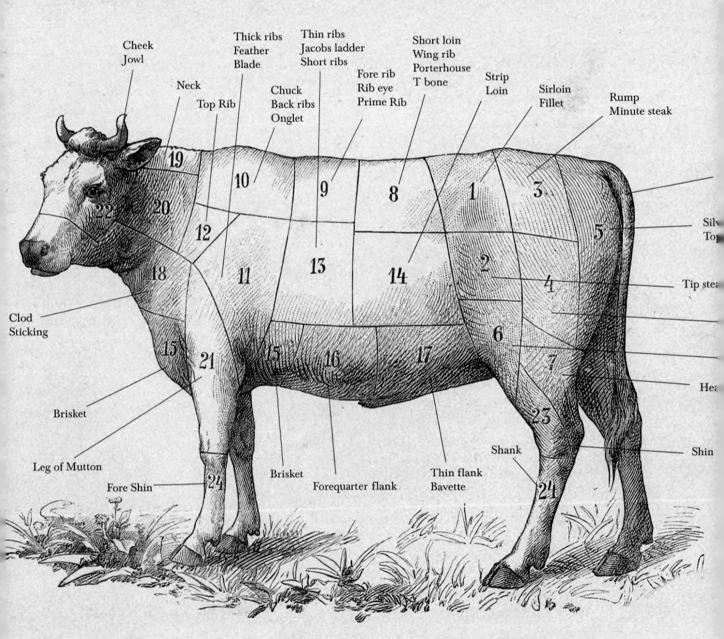

HOW TO COOK A BRISKET

Time Commitment: Two days.

Easy Way Out: Pre-cooked brisket from the grocery store. (Store-bought is not terrific on its own, but it will get the job done in composed dishes or sandwiches).

Along with pork and chicken, brisket is one of the three centerpieces of the OMC's menu. It is a foundational item for barbecue. Cooking it can get fairly technical, so many of you may not ever smoke one. But for those who do, the rewards are endless. To keep the focus on the beef, the OMC likes to leave brisket as close to natural as possible. Sauce it up on your plate, but try it pure first.

Ingredients
1 beef brisket (8–13 pounds)
1 cup brisket rub (page 7)
Mustard mix (½ cup mustard + 2 Tbsp pickle juice)

In The Smoker
1 log sugar maple
1 log oak
3 gallons water

Instructions follow

* Read more about smokers on page 113

Brisket Instructions

Typical beef brisket

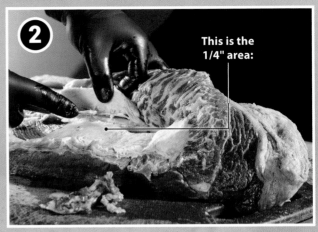

This is the 1/4" area:

Trim brisket fat to ¼ inch evenly.

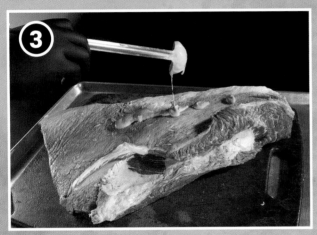

Coat the outside of the brisket with mustard mix.

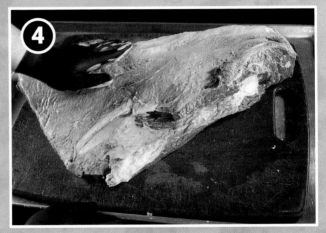

Err on the side of too much mustard mix rather than not enough

After coating with the mustard mix, rub the outside of the brisket liberally with the dry rub.

Be sure to coat the sides

Flip the brisket: now repeat coating the back and sides with the mustard and rub.

Well-coated brisket, ready for the next step:

Place brisket in the fridge to rest overnight.

In the morning, heat the smoker to 230°, add water to bottom of the smoker (we use 3 gallons), and 1 log of oak and 1 log of sugar maple.

When smoker is hot and ready, place brisket on rack, with fat cap on top.

Smoke brisket for 6–8 hours, or until the beef reaches 170°. Remove.

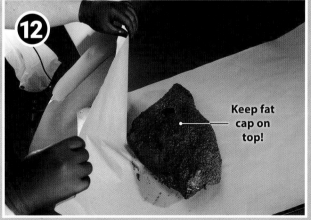
Keep fat cap on top!

Wrap in brown butcher paper, make 2–3 wraps and keep the fat cap on top (fat needs to run down into the meat, not into the paper).

Finished wrap should look like this

Paper needs to be *tight* against the brisket.

Once wrapped, return brisket to smoker to finish.

Check temperature hourly until internal temp reaches 200° at the point (see next step).

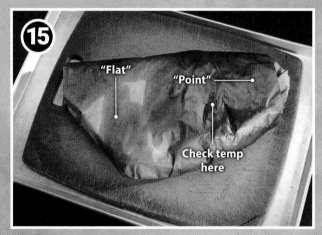

"Flat"

"Point"

Check temp here

When point of brisket reaches 200° (no more, no less) remove brisket. Let brisket rest 30–40 minutes.

Brisket should remain wrapped until the rest period has elapsed.

Slice away!

The finished meat should easily pull apart!

LOADED MAC AND CHEESE

Here's something for when you're too sophisticated to just eat Mac and Cheese, but not *so* sophisticated that you'll refuse it. Sautéed mushrooms, onions, and bacon add some texture and any time you can dump brisket on pasta...well, that's a good day.

Yield: 4-6 Servings

Ingredients
1 lb uncooked rotini pasta
3 cups cheese sauce (page 17)
4 strips cooked bacon, chopped
1 onion, chopped
1 cup mushrooms, sliced
20 oz chopped brisket
½ cup shredded cheese
butter or oil for sautéing

Instruction
Cook pasta according to package directions and saute the onions in butter or oil for a few minutes at medium heat. Throw in the mushrooms and keep sautéing. Meanwhile, warm up your cheese sauce and brisket on the stovetop (make sure to not heat the brisket so much that you dry it out). Drain the pasta, put all ingredients together in a bowl with bacon, and top with cheese. Bon appetit!

Did you notice the bacon? Never skip the bacon.

Yield: 12 Tacos

These are a hybrid between a Minnesota style taco and a traditional Mexican taco. People up north tend to like larger, overstuffed tacos with white flour tortillas instead of a smaller corn tortilla. As for the fillings, we're using brisket here, but you could use pulled chicken or pork just as well. It's fun to do these a la carte style where people can build their own.

Ingredients
12 6-inch flour tortillas
1 cup jalapeño lime slaw
   (page 28)
1/2 cup pico de gallo
1/4 cup pickled jalapeños
   (page 32 or use store-bought)
1/2 cup brined onions (page 31
   or use store-bought)
1 lb meat of choice
2 whole limes, cut into wedges
Cilantro

Instructions
When you have tacos and a crowd, it's easiest to make them buffet style. Set up a station for tortillas, then meat, then toppings. Or if you're trying to encourage vegetable consumption, put the meat last! There's no wrong way to eat tacos.

The lime isn't there just for looks: squeeze it over the taco

Brisket shown — works as well with pulled chicken or pork

We use wheat taco shells but corn shells work just as well

This is Comfort Food 101: a tender buttery brioche bun, smokey brisket, and melty cheddar on top. Pop on a little tomato jam to liven it up, and you've got the perfect sandwich.

Yield: 1 Sandwich

Ingredients
Brioche bun
5 oz chopped brisket
1 slice cheddar cheese
2 oz tomato onion jam (page 12)

Instructions
Toast brioche bun. Gently reheat brisket in a pan and top with cheese, warm a little more until cheese is melted. Smear some jam on the bun, top with meat, and eat.

You can also melt cheese under a broiler

Tomato onion jam

HAYSTACK BRISKET

This brisket sandwich actually came from Joe Slack, the pitmaster at Red Wagon BBQ in Waco, Texas. After we were done eating, Joe told us they take chopped brisket, slaw, and crispy onions to make a good sandwich. He also builds guitars by hand, so the man is clearly an artist.

Yield: 1 Sandwich

Ingredients
Brioche bun
Haystack onions (page 28)
2 pieces Bibb lettuce
2 oz Classic Coleslaw
   (page 23)
5 oz chopped brisket
2 oz haystack onions

Instructions
Take the coleslaw out of the fridge half an hour before serving to take the edge off the chill. Toast brioche bun. Gently reheat brisket in a pan (you'd hate to accidentally overcook it). Top with crispy haystack onions and enjoy while listening to some old-fashioned country music.

Haystack
Onions,
page 28

Quick, easy, you can pack it to go and make anytime. Leftover brisket chopped up with cilantro lime slaw and a little Alabama White Sauce is tasty without being overly messy. Finally: barbecue you can eat on an airplane.

Yield: 1 Wrap

Ingredients
12 inch flour tortilla, warm
6 pieces Bibb lettuce
5 oz brisket
4 oz jalapeño lime slaw
   (page 28)
3 oz pico de gallo
1 slice cheddar
2 oz Alabama White Sauce
   (page 10)

Instructions
Wrap it all up in the tortilla like a burrito. Start with the lettuce and pile everything on top of that. Boom! Brisket wrap.

Alabama White Sauce: use it as a dip (or drizzle a line down the filling before wrapping).

Oink moo cluck in one burger! The OMC doesn't do burgers anymore because there was a brief period where burger was hard to get and they got rid of a grill, but that doesn't mean it has to define you. You're a champion. And you're gonna make this burger great.

Yield: 1 Sandwich

Ingredients
Brioche bun
Haystack onions, (page 28)
2 pieces of Bibb lettuce
1 slice of tomato
8 oz burger patty
1 oz honey BBQ sauce
(page 10)
1 slice cheddar cheese
2 oz pulled pork
1 over easy egg
2 oz haystack onions
Pickles

Instructions
Toast brioche bun. Grill the burger, ideally over a wood fire or charcoal but we're not going to report you if you use a propane grill. Shortly before it's done, put the honey BBQ sauce on, then the cheese, so the BBQ caramelizes just a bit as the cheese melts. Meanwhile, fry the egg in a pan and gently heat the pulled pork in a saute pan. (Microwaves have a tendency to dry meat out). Assemble ingredients and serve.

Haystack Onions, page 28

Yes, a fried egg

Pulled Pork (of course)

Burger patty

CLUCK

Chicken has so many things going for it, it's hard to know where to start. It's one of the least expensive, widely available meats out there. It's relatively nutritious, especially the white meat without skin. And because the wings and tenders are thinner than, say, a brisket, they're comparatively quick to smoke. Versatile and delicious, it's one of the easiest ways to get started with Southern cooking.

And then there's fried chicken. *Nothing* compares to fried chicken.

Thigh

Wing

1

3

4

2

Breast

Drumstick

HOW TO COOK CHICKEN
(Wings, Tenders, Whole Smoked)

Marinating chicken makes it incredibly tender and moist, and gives you more room to maneuver when cooking. The richness of buttermilk and a touch of heat from Tabasco make this stand out.

Time Commitment: A few hours

Easy Way Out: For store-bought tenders, you can skip this step if you'd like. For wings, you really should marinate if you're going to smoke or fry.

Ingredients:

1 lb chicken wings or tenders	2 cups buttermilk	2 Tbsp Tabasco sauce	½ tsp salt

Add ingredients to a bowl and mix well. If you're making a smaller quantity, use a Ziploc bag.

Add raw chicken to bowl or bag and toss to coat.

The two-step dip and dredge process gives you a thicker, breadier crust, because the dip helps the dredge stick to the chicken. Plus, the egg gives added heft. You could even call it "chicken, past and present" since you're using the early "egg" version of a chicken and the later "meat" version of a chicken in the same dish. Should you call it that? No, but you still could.

Time Commitment: Minutes.

Easy Way Out: Buy pre-cooked from the store and use a good homemade sauce.

Ingredients:

1 lb chicken tenders, marinated (see previous page)

Dip:
2 cups 2% milk
4 eggs
1 Tbsp Tabasco

Dredge:
2 cups all-purpose flour
2 Tbsp salt
3/4 tsp black pepper
1/8 tsp cayenne

INSTRUCTIONS

Place flour, seasoned salt, and black pepper in a separate bowl and mix well. Place milk, eggs, and tabasco in a medium bowl and mix well.

First coat the tenders with the dredge.

Then dunk them in the dip.

Dredge them again and lay on baking sheet, ready for frying!

5

325

Allow enough room, do not overflow your fry pan.

Heat oil to 325º.

6

Place breaded tender into hot oil.

7

Internal temp should measure at least 165º

Fry to golden brown.

Toss tenders in Nashville Hot sauce (page 7), or Georgia Gold BBQ (page 10).

Chicken Tenders served with Blue Cheese Dressing, page 14

Smoked chicken wings are the ideal party appetizer and one of the faster things you can make in a smoker. Taking the extra time to smoke wings takes them from your typical wing to something that's extraordinary.

Yield: As many as you want

Time Commitment: A few hours.

Easy Way Out: If you don't smoke, they'll still be pretty good, just not "extraordinary". Marinating makes a big difference and so does the sauce you use!

Ingredients:	**Smoker**
Marinated chicken wings	1 log maple
(You can smoke as many as fit	3 gallons of water
into your smoker)	
Oil for the fryer	

INSTRUCTIONS

Remove marinated wings from marinade and place on sheet pan.

Place in smoker at 230° until internal temp reaches 165°. Remove when done and allow to cool properly on sheet trays.

Allow enough room; do not overflow your fry pan.

350

Heat oil to 350° in a fry pan.

Add wings to fry pan gently. Cook until internal temperature is 165° and skin is crispy.

WHOLE SMOKED CHICKEN

A whole smoked chicken is great for Oktoberfest or Thanksgiving, but the uses don't end there. Make a quesadilla out of it, shred the meat for tacos, plop it on a sandwich, or just dunk it in your favorite barbecue sauce.

Yield:
1 Chicken

Time Commitment: Minutes.

Easy Way Out: Buy pre-cooked from the store and use a good homemade sauce.

Ingredients:	Smoker
1 whole chicken	2 logs sugar maple
2 Tbsp chicken rub (page 7)	3 gallons water

INSTRUCTIONS

Rub whole chicken down with the chicken rub.

Ensure smoker is preheated to 240° with sugar maple wood.

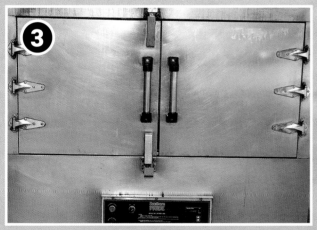

Place whole rub chickens into the smoker at 240° for 1–2 hours or until chicken has reached an internal temp of 165°.

When chicken is finished, serve or cool to store.

BBQ RANCH SALAD

Vegetables aren't just a punitive, ascetic ritual you go through to satisfy your doctor. They offer crunch, refreshment, and plenty of flavor of their own. This Tex-Mex inspired salad hits like something from a San Diego taco truck with pico de gallo, corn relish, and cheddar cheese taking care of all your drive-through cravings. One theme in this book is setting you free from culinary constraints. So if you want pulled pork or chopped brisket instead of pulled chicken, go for it. Switch out the sauce for a dressing. Really, these recipes are just templates.

Yield: 1 Salad

Ingredients
3 cups salad mix
3 oz pico de gallo
3 oz Corn Relish
    (page 30)
2 oz cheddar cheese
5 oz pulled chicken
    heated up
2 oz Honey BBQ sauce
    (page 10)
4 tortilla chips
Ranch dressing
    to serve

Instructions
Mix first three ingredients. Top with cheese, chicken, and honey BBQ. Garnish with tortilla chips and serve with ranch dressing.

SMOKED CHICKEN CLUB WRAP

Gourmands will note that with bacon, lettuce, tomato, and mayo, this has the flavors of a classic BLT. Alongside chicken (or whatever meat you like) and cheddar cheese, it's a hearty wrap with the right balance of crunch and chew.

Yield: 1 Wrap

Ingredients
12 inch flour tortilla,
    warm
6 pieces Bibb lettuce
2 oz diced tomatoes
1 strip cooked bacon
1 slice cheddar
2 oz mayo
5 oz pulled chicken

Instructions
Wrap it all up like a burrito. Now you've got it! This is a cold wrap so no need to heat, beyond slightly warming the tortilla to make it easier to fold. If you wrap it up in aluminum foil you have a great on-the-go lunch.

Yield: 1 Sandwich

A restaurant is 98% hard work and 2% coming up with ridiculous names for things. You sauce it yourself, so this sandwich is very kid-friendly. Or if you're like my (Robert's) kid, you can take every single ingredient apart, eat one of them, and then run off to play. But I digress.

Ingredients
Brioche bun
5 oz pulled chicken
1 slice cheddar cheese
1 slice bacon

Instructions
Toast bun. Fry bacon. Separately top chicken with cheese and gently warm in a pan until just warm (you don't want to dry it out). Or if you're fancy, instead of a pan, pop it under a broiler until cheese is melty. Top with bacon and eat.

Yield: 1 Sandwich

The sandwich that set the world on fire. And Robert's mouth. And Louis' stomach. It's eye-wateringly hot, but it burns delightfully. There's a richness from the oil, and a crunch from the fried batter, and a subtle sweetness from the spice blend that gives this chicken lots of flavor!

The dish has been around since the 1930s but the present spice blend seems to have been invented in the 1970s by the family of Andre Prince Jeffries, owner of Prince's Hot Chicken Shack in Nashville. It's become iconic and spawned variations including Hot Fish. Tread carefully and use blue cheese or ranch to cut the pain.

Ingredients
Brioche bun
2 pieces Bibb lettuce
1 slice tomato
3 chicken tenders tossed in
   Nashville Hot seasoning
   (page 77)

Instructions
Toast your brioche bun and assemble the lettuce and tomato. Get your blue cheese or ranch cup ready (this is not mandatory, but it's highly recommended!) Then, and only then, fry your chicken. Note that Nashville Hot is NOT a spice blend you put on before frying, it's more of an oil-based sauce. You fry your chicken the normal way first, then add the Nashville Hot after. (See page 7 for instructions). Enjoy!

Classic coleslaw, page 23

Blue cheese Dressing

This is the sweet version of Nashville Hot. Marinating and hand breading chicken tenders, rolling them through the honey mustard sauce, and putting them on bread with a little lettuce and tomato makes for a pleasant sandwich that will bring you back to happy fourth grade memories.

Yield: 1 Sandwich

Ingredients
Brioche bun
2 pieces Bibb lettuce
1 slice tomato
3 chicken tenders tossed in Georgia Gold sauce (page 77)

Instructions
Toast your brioche bun and assemble the lettuce and tomato. Make sure your side dishes and drinks are ready. Warm the sauce just to room temp (microwave for very short bursts and stir, or just leave out on the counter for half an hour). Then, and only then, get going on the part where you fry the chicken. You want that puppy searing hot before you get it on the sandwich—with anything fried, fresh is absolutely best. Enjoy!

KENTUCKY HOT BROWN

Yield: 8 Sandwiches

The Kentucky Hot Brown gets its name from the Brown Hotel in Kentucky. Everyone would be out dancing, partying, and drinking bourbon. Then they'd want something to eat afterwards. The OMC serves the classic version where you brine and pull a turkey then top it with a Parmesan gravy. Brining a turkey is beyond the scope of this cookbook, but you can make a delicious sandwich with pulled chicken instead!

Ingredients
8 slices of Texas toast
4 cups of hot brown gravy (page 17)
8 strips of chopped bacon
1 cup diced tomato
20 oz smoked pulled chicken
4 oz shredded Parmesan

Instructions
Put bread down in 6"x9" pan (these are open faced sandwiches).
Top with chicken, bacon, tomato and gravy, then Parmesan. Broil until just browned.

CHICKEN/TURKEY STACKER

Yield: 1 Sandwich

Thanksgiving on a bun! Rhubarb and cranberry jam is a tangy accent for smoked chicken, crunchy coleslaw, and fried onions. You can make this with chicken or turkey.

Ingredients
Brioche bun
2 pieces Bibb lettuce
5 oz smoked chicken or turkey
2 oz classic coleslaw (page 23)
Haystack onions (page 28)
Squirt of rhubarb and cranberry jam (page 14)

Instructions
Toast bun. Top with lettuce, then coleslaw, then chicken or turkey. Add haystack onions. Smear jam on top.

Chicken/Turkey Stacker

Pretending You Can't Walk, Slashed Tires and Raising Kids
GROWING UP AT A FAMILY RESTAURANT

When OMC partner Louis Hanson was a toddler, he struggled to walk. So his mom Jaima carried him everywhere, and often worried something was wrong. Then, one day, she came around the corner and caught him walking perfectly. He had been pretending the whole time. Kid just wanted to be carried. "He's a really determined guy," Jaima says.

You need that kind of determination in the restaurant business. Far from just cooking, you've got to be able to handle customer service, tax law, employees calling you from jail, etc. And sewer backups! Don't forget sewer backups.

But Jeff (now also a partner at OMC) and Louis had their fun moments too. One day when they were in high school while working at the restaurant, they were screwing around with the computer system. Jeff changed Louis' password and locked him out of the system. So Louis changed Jeff's password and locked Jeff out. The system froze, locking up

Tom and a young Louis

the entire restaurant on a busy Saturday morning. The two were laughing about it when Louis' dad Tom stormed in.

"You think that's funny?" Tom asked, in a tone used by dads everywhere. "You know what would be *really* funny? If I go into the parking lot and slash your car tires right now." The room got quiet. "We were worried he was actually going to do it," Louis recalls.

Fortunately, no tires were slashed that day. But maneuvering through tricky shifts, keeping your head about you when things are going crazy, that's just part of working the line.

Jaima says that from an early age, her son didn't give up.

Louis showing off his early riding skills.

"When he was 3, he wanted to ride a bike. Normally you can't ride a bike that age, but he was all dressed up in his snowmobile suit," she recalls. "Tom finally let him go, and he rode all around the park until he fell down. He was an 'I'm gonna stick this through and see this out' kind of kid.

Tom and Jaima have worked in restaurants since they were young. That meant long hours, but also a more casual work environment for Louis, his brother Tony, and his sister Valerie.

"It just became natural to us, being involved," Valerie says. "When my mom worked at Augustino's we'd bike down there, eat lunch, and hang out at the boardwalk."

Louis started bussing tables at 16 and just worked his way up. Between sports and the restaurant, he was finding a calling. "He was always a hard worker—on things that he enjoyed," Valerie says. "He'd rather be doing other stuff than homework. Sports, he liked a lot."

Louis' parents used to take turns—one would work while the other watched the kids. Louis and his wife Ashley now have a similar setup. Ashley serves at the Duluth Grill for the breakfast shift, allowing her to be home with their two sons later in the day. Louis says at least one of his sons is thinking of following in his footsteps. "It's long hours but you get an immediate tangible result every day," Louis says. "You're working with people, and it becomes addicting after a while."

Louis prepping holiday cookies in the Embers kitchen (with Jaima in the background), circa 2006.

Now, the kid who wanted to be carried everywhere, and that goofy high school friend—now a partner in the family business—are carrying the weight of the three family restaurants. And Louis' sister Valerie, who helped put together the dessert menu at OMC, manages the family business across the street—Corktown Deli. It's "all in the family" and the family keeps growing.

"I'm so proud of them," Jaima says. "They have really good work ethics." OMC

OTHER PROTEINS

Catfish don't oink. Salmon don't moo. And lentils don't cluck...unless something has gone seriously wrong with your lentils. There are proteins in this world other than pigs, cows, and chickens, and the OMC didn't want to leave them out entirely. This section finds us in the "other" side of the menu. Prepared with just as much skill as the classics of barbecue, these fish and veggie dishes are a fun change of pace and a way to satisfy diners who don't eat meat.

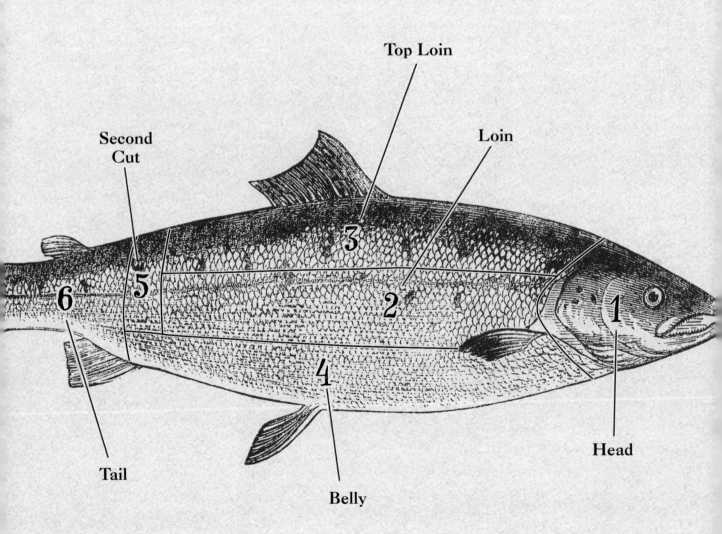

Top Loin

Second
Cut

Loin

3

5

2

6

1

4

Tail

Belly

Head

HOW TO COOK SALMON

SMOKED SALMON

Brining salmon seasons the meat, improving the flavor. This process also partially dissolves muscle fibers to form water-retaining gel and helps prevent the flesh from drying out.

Time Commitment:
Done in 1 day plus

Ingredients:
2 quarts water
2¼ cups kosher salt
1 cup brown sugar
   packed

black pepper
1–2 whole salmon
   filets

1

Stir until salt and sugar are fully dissolved.

Combine all ingredients except salmon in large pot and bring to soft boil.

2   Brine for two hours

Once brine is cool, place salmon and brine into a container. (Make sure it's submerged).

3   Wipe off brine with gloved hand

Place salmon on a wire rack and rinse filet thoroughly with cold water. Allow to dry overnight in the fridge for 8–16 hours.

4

Place in convection oven under low fan and dry until filet begins to "sweat".

Continued

When dry, rub "sweat" over filet so the pepper will stick.

A "pellicle"—a sticky surface gel—forms on the surface. Rub this in. This helps retain moisture and aids smoke penetration.

Remove from screen, place on oiled smoker racks, and sprinkle with black pepper.

Drain water from smoker, move wood to firebox (pieces no more than 2" diameter).

Once fish temp reaches 140° turn up smoker to 200°F until fish is fully cooked (145°, approximately 25 minutes)

Looking for some new ideas for smoked salmon? This wrap brings in enough new flavors to jazz things up without losing the richness of the fish. Crunchy from lettuce and brined onions, creamy from salmon dip and malt vinegar aioli—the balance is perfect! This is a sandwich for romance, a sandwich for hope and joy. If it a wrap is a sandwich that is (it's an open debate online).

Yield: 1 Wrap

Ingredients

Warm tortilla
6 pieces of Bibb lettuce
2 oz diced tomato
2 oz brined onion (page 31)
1 scoop salmon pimento dip (page 42)
3 oz smoked salmon
2 oz malt vinegar aioli (page 15)

Instructions

Warm the tortilla and smear with salmon pimento dip.
Top with lettuce and tomato, then salmon and onion.
Drizzle on malt vinegar aioli. Roll it all up and enjoy.

Save your leftover salmon for this dish — like turkey sandwiches after Thanksgiving.

Malt Vinegar Aioli, page 15

Every region has its fish. Except for deserts. And isolated mountain communities. And totally landlocked regions with little water. Okay, so most regions have their fish. The southern classic is catfish, which is meaty and goes well with spice. This couldn't-be-simpler recipe also works with other fish like walleye or panfish. Bring the dredge on your next fishing trip for a little BBQ kick.

Yield:
4 Servings

Ingredients
4 filets of catfish
1½ cups catfish dredge (page 6)

Instructions
Coat catfish in catfish dredge and fry until golden brown.

Malt vinegar aioli, page 15

Beef fat fries, page 29

Fried Catfish

Surf and turf, without the turf! Or the surf, since catfish are a freshwater fish. At any event, this fish sandwich is a tasty classic done right. Malt aioli is a richer, thicker version of the dipping vinegar you'll find at east coast French fry shops. It's a different twist on tartar sauce that brings the whole sandwich together.

Yield: 1 Serving

Ingredients
Brioche bun
2 pieces Bibb lettuce
1 slice tomato
5 oz portion of catfish, dredged
  and ready to fry
2 oz malt vinegar aioli
  (page 15)

Instructions
Toast bun. Put on lettuce, tomato, and a smear of malt vinegar aioli. Then, and only then, pop that catfish in a fryer filled with hot oil. (A pan could work too). You don't want to mess around with fried fish as it gets cool in about half a second and then it doesn't taste good anymore. Fresh fried is the only solution.

Malt vinegar aioli (page 15) on the toasted bun

Mellow and a little tangy, Gouda plays well with smoky salmon. Capers add a touch of elegance, brined onion brings the vinegar, and pico de gallo and corn relish stand in for dressing. This salad is crisp and refreshing, but doesn't sacrifice richness to get there.

Yield: 1 Salad

Ingredients
3 cups salad mix
3 oz pico de gallo
3 oz Corn Relish (page 30)
2 oz Gouda cheese
2 oz Brined Onion (page 31)
3 oz salmon filet
1 oz fried capers

Instructions
The capers don't need to be fried, but pan frying them with a bit of olive oil gives them a bit of crunch. Garnish with lemon and put your choice of dressing on the side.

Some of the best artists work under constraints. Finding something to impress vegetarians in the context of a barbecue restaurant was a difficult task, but these Vegetarian Sloppy Joes get the job done and then some! LOADED with flavor from Cuba's "holy trinity" of onion, garlic, and bell pepper fried in olive oil, the lentils and quinoa then get dosed up with chili powder and paprika before an all-American hit of ketchup and mustard. Is it over yet? No—apple cider vinegar, brown sugar and black pepper throw a "pot roast" twist at the whole affair.

Yield: 8 Joes

Ingredients

3 cups lentils (cooked)
1½ cup quinoa (cooked)
1/4 cup olive oil
2½ cups yellow onion (small diced)
2½ cups green pepper (chopped)
2½ tsp garlic (minced)
4½ tsp chili powder
6 Tbsp ketchup
1 tsp smoked paprika
3/4 cup yellow mustard
3½ cup diced tomato

6 Tbsp brown sugar
2½ Tbsp apple cider vinegar
1½ tsp salt
1/2 tsp black pepper
8 Buns for serving
Optional Brined Onions (page 31)
Optional Pickled Jalapeños (page 32)
Optional pickle slices

Instructions

Heat olive oil in a large pot over medium heat. Add the onion and pepper, and cook for 5 to 8 minutes, or until the onion is soft and clear, stirring frequently. Add the garlic, chili, paprika, and mustard, and continue cooking for another minute or two, until the garlic is fragrant.

Add the lentils, quinoa, diced tomatoes, brown sugar, ketchup, apple cider vinegar, salt, and pepper. Bring the mixture to a simmer. Simmer for about 20 minutes.

For each sandwich, assemble sloppy joe with bun, a scoop of sloppy joe mix, then brined onions and pickled jalapeños. Add pickle slices to taste.

Lentils are a great source of plant protein, and so is quinoa. Together they pack a superfood punch!

COCKTAILS

This cocktail section can be enjoyed on three levels. Some of the drinks (like the Karin's Cup and the Watermelon Gin) are single sized. Others, like the Margaritas, are already batch sized for a party. And finally, the cocktail tips show you it's possible to scale a recipe up or down—and even make your own signature creation.

This cocktail came from the Noble Pour, a short-lived but glorious cocktail concept that was later folded into the OMC. The "Karin" is Karin Kraemer, a local artist who made the great skull mugs it's traditionally served in.

Yield: 1 Serving

Ingredients
1½ oz mezcal (we like Cruz de Fuego)
1/2 oz Bodegas Oliver vermouth (Punt e Mes)
1/2 oz lime juice
1/2 oz simple syrup

Instructions
Shake, serve over ice in skull cups.

WATERMELON GIN

Here's a drink built up from first principles. Watermelon juice is light and fruity, so it offsets the herbal flavor of Yellow Chartreuse. Midori, a melon liqueur, brings it back in the sweet direction, so that's tempered with the tangy juniper notes of gin. Finish it off with a flourish of elderflower and you've got a complex but rewarding tipple. Ohhh, I cringe just reading the word "tipple". And here I chose to write it.

Yield: 1 Serving

Ingredients
1½ oz gin
1/4 oz Midori
1/4 oz Yellow Chartreuse
1/4 oz St Germain elderflower liqueur
2 oz fresh pureed watermelon juice

Instructions
Stir with ice in a mixing cup.

Everything old is new again: the old fashioned is now the drink of choice for trendy Millennials, and a great all-around cocktail for sipping. This is more of an independent sipper before or after your meal. While it's probably too heavy to complement barbecue, it's certainly a nice way to start a party.

Ingredients
1 liter Bulleit Bourbon
9 fl oz Amaro di Angostura
3/4 cup sugar
6 fl oz hot water

Yield: 12 Generous Servings

Instructions
Dissolve sugar in water. Add Amaro and mix well. Add bourbon and mix well. Chill.

Premake this batch recipe so you can enjoy the party: just pour over ice and enjoy!

COCKTAIL TIPS

Cocktails can feel intimidating, but if you understand a few basic principles, they're fairly straightforward.

First and foremost, cocktails are about ratios. The classic "sour" ratio is 2:1:1. That's two parts alcohol, one part lemon or lime juice, and 1 part sweet, like syrup or triple sec. Want a margarita? Tequila, lime, agave syrup. A maple whiskey sour? Whiskey, lemon, maple syrup. Want a mojito? Rum, lime, simple syrup (and muddle a few mint leaves in there). Or how about the "2:1:2"—two ounces of alcohol, one ounce of vermouth, two dashes of bitters? That's a Manhattan (with bourbon and sweet vermouth) or a Martini (with gin and dry vermouth).

The beauty of a ratio is that you can make cocktails as large or small as you want, so that 2:1:2? It could be 2 ounces or 2 cups, depending on how much you'd like to make! Go easy with bitters on larger batches; like salt, they scale unpredictably.

To invent your own cocktail, pick a favorite ratio and mix and match from there. Or start with a recipe you like, then swap out like-for-like and see how it goes (for example, swap simple syrup for equal parts maple syrup, or lemon for lime, or whiskey with rum).

Continued

MARGARITA (BATCH)

Did you know Jimmy Buffett actually found his "long-lost shaker of salt" a year after Margaritaville came out? But by then, the song was so popular as it was that he had to keep singing those same lyrics. None of this anecdote was true, but we needed to fill space and you already know what a margarita is.

Yield: 12 Cocktails

Ingredients
1 liter 1800 Silver Tequila
11 fl oz Triple Sec
Just over 1 cup sugar
18 fl oz hot water
16 fl oz fresh lime juice

Instructions
Dissolve sugar in hot water. Add lime juice and mix well. Add Triple Sec (or any other orange liqueur including Grand Marnier, Cointreau, O3, or Curacao) and tequila and mix well. Chill.

Traditionally rimmed with salt and a wedge of lime. May *not* be served in a red Solo cup...unless you're wearing Crocs.

COCKTAIL TIPS, CONTINUED

Now let's look at technique. Shaken or stirred? James Bond quotes aside, you normally wouldn't shake a martini. Booze-forward cocktails with no citrus should be stirred with ice, and cocktails with citrus or juices should be shaken with ice to aerate them and soften the citrus. The ice you use is important, too. Bars will often leave ice out in a bin behind the counter (and it's tempting to do the same at a barbecue) but over the course of the evening, the ice itself gets honeycombed and structurally weaker. You want large, cold ice cubes straight from the freezer. Ice is supposed to chill and dilute a drink, but ice that's too warm will melt too much and make your cocktails too weak.

A classic bourbon sour with a little twist from the honey. If a couple of you wanted these frothy, you could pour some into a cocktail shaker, shake it with ice, strain it, pour it back into the shaker, and then shake it again with a couple of egg whites. That's called a "reverse dry shake" and it works quite well!

Yield: 12 Generous Servings

Ingredients
1 liter Cabin Still Bourbon
6.5 fl oz hot water
6.5 fl oz honey
13 fl oz fresh lemon juice

Instructions
Mix honey with hot water and stir until dissolved. Add lemon juice and mix well. Add bourbon and mix well. Chill.

Customizing in action: a simple bourbon sour is transformed by swapping simple syrup for a bit of honey.

RED SANGRIA (BATCH)

Ahhhh....sangria! The classic Spanish punch goes well with any sort of roast meat. Feel free to use a bottom-shelf wine for this puppy, between the fruit and honey you'll disguise the flavor plenty. See, how many cookbooks are ever this honest with you???

Yield: 1 Gallon

Ingredients
3 liters red wine
4 ounces honey
3 cups pomegranate juice
6 ounces Rose's Lime Juice
2 sliced lemons (in rounds)
2 sliced limes (in rounds)

Instructions
Mix first four ingredients (all but lemons and limes) and whisk thoroughly. Add lemons and limes. Chill. Strain after 24 hours. (You can drink it earlier but it's nice to make it a day in advance so the lemons and limes can infuse it).

A fun garnish nicely tops off a drink.

Crisp and refreshing as a jump in the lake. (Can you tell we're from Minnesota?) Alcohol dehydrates, lemonade rehydrates, and so our final "cocktail" recipe is a classic summertime drink with not a drop of booze. Plus, you could always make this a cocktail by throwing in some vodka. In fact, if you reduced the water and added some whiskey, you'd have a whiskey sour. Or, if you didn't add alcohol, you could swap lemons for limes to make limeade. See, here we go improvising again. It's so easy!

Ingredients
2 cups water
2 cups sugar
2 cups lemon juice

**Yield:
12 Cups**

8 more cups cold water

. . . .

Instructions
Add 2 cups water, 2 cups sugar, and two cups lemon juice to pan and bring to a boil.

Finish with adding 8 cups of cold water. Stir.

The Right Meat
THE PHILOSOPHY BEHIND THE OMC'S INGREDIENTS

In the beginning, the OMC spent five to six months researching to find the right product. Sometimes it was challenging!

PORK

Premier Proteins, which is non-antibiotic, had a really nice pork, but their selection was really limited. The OMC team was always challenging themselves to find a great product and keep quality high.

They settled on Compart Family Farms, a big family farm that really cares about their product. "It's not one person who tried it out and picked a different brand," Louis says. "Everyone, when testing side by side, agreed on this."

It has a dark red coloring and the fat content is nice. Cooked side by side with a commodity raised hog, you can instantly tell the difference.

In fact, they liked it so much they even switched sister restaurant Corktown Deli's hams and porchettas over to Compart Farms.

BEEF

There's a big debate between grass-fed and angus. The OMC tried them all. Grass-fed brisket turned out to be a little lean, but Hereford had great marbling and moisture content.

But in a region with a less-developed meat industry like northern Minnesota, it was hard to use a local farmer. That's because scalability was an issue.

"We use 100 brisket a week," Louis says, "That's 50 heads of cattle. Then the farmers are asking 'what do you want to do with the rest of it?' And we're like 'no, we just want the brisket'."

So the OMC went with a larger national company with a good product. Of course, as a smaller-scale local cook, you have the option of going with anyone you like!

CHICKEN

The OMC uses Gerber Amish raised chickens. It's a high quality product available at scale. Louis says the same debate with beef applies to chicken—the OMC may use 300 chickens a week.

"If we go through a local person, they say 'yeah, I'll give you 300 birds, but they're frozen',"Louis says. "Then we have 300 chickens we need to thaw. Space and time are an issue."

On a smaller scale feel free to hit up the farmer's market. If you're using 300 chickens a week, we recommend Gerber Amish chickens. OMC

BAKED GOODS & DESSERTS

OMC's desserts were originally called "The Tail of The Pig". Not the main event, but a pleasant ending if you want a little something extra. Jaima, who loves desserts, thought it would be fun to bring a Southern feel to the end of the menu with whoopie pies, toffee bundt cakes, and Hummingbird Cake. These desserts are easy to prep ahead of time and keep in the freezer so you don't feel overwhelmed on Barbecue Day. And if you just aren't up for making more food, you can always do what the OMC did when it started running out of kitchen space. Simply tell your guests "let's all go out for ice cream!"

Hummingbird Cake,
page 110

PS. Barbecue is a lot of smoking, a lot of sauces, and a lot of side dishes, but not a ton of baking. So while we didn't know exactly where to put our cornbread and biscuits recipes...we decided to put them here. Consider this the "carb section"!

Jaima read a bunch of magazines to see what's popular down south. Whoopie Pies were one of the first things that came up. Soft and chocolatey, the individual layers are more like a cake than a pie. Then they sandwich a marshmallow cream filling. They went over really well, especially in the neighborhood. The owner of Frost River started ordering them in huge quantities to share with his family!

Yield: 18 Pies

Ingredients

Pie Shells

1/2 cup butter, softened
1 cup brown sugar
1 egg
1 tsp vanilla
2 cups all-purpose flour

1/3 cup cocoa powder
1 tsp baking powder
1 tsp baking soda
1/2 tsp salt
1 cup buttermilk

Filling

1 cup butter, softened
1½ cups confectioner's sugar
Pinch salt

7 oz marshmallow crème
1 tsp vanilla

Instructions

Pie Instructions

Whip butter and brown sugar in a mixer. Add eggs and vanilla. Mix well. In a separate bowl, mix flour, cocoa powder, baking powder, and baking soda. Add dry mix and buttermilk slowly (alternating between the two).

If you have whoopie pie pans, spray them and spoon batter into pans evenly (#24 scoop). After pans are filled, evenly press each pie before baking. If you don't have whoopie pie pans, butter a couple of large baking sheets and spoon 1/8 cup mounds of batter an inch and a half apart.

Bake in oven at 325 degrees for 6 min with no fan. Take out of pans and place on sheet tray and let cool.

Filling Instructions

In mixer, add butter, salt, and confectioner's sugar. Mix well. Add marshmallow crème and mix well.

Add vanilla and mix until fully incorporated.

TOFFEE BUNDT CAKE

With BBQ you control what you can. You can make a batch of these and hold them in the freezer, then pull out as needed for special occasions. Besides, Louis thinks cake tastes better when it's frozen and warmed up again!

Yield: 13 Mini Cakes About 3" Diameter

Ingredients
5 eggs
3 cups flour
1 tsp baking powder
2 cups brown sugar
1 cup sugar
1/2 tsp salt
1 cup pecans (toasted)
1½ cups butter
1 cup milk
8 oz toffee bits

Instructions
Whip butter until creamy. Add both sugars and mix well. Add eggs one at a time and mix well. In a separate bowl, mix flour, baking powder, and salt. Add dry mix and milk slowly to butter-sugar-egg bowl, alternating between the two. Fold in toffee bits and toasted pecans. Spray mini bundt pans. Add 3 golfball-sized scoops to each slot in pan. Once all pans are filled press each evenly. Bake in convection oven at 325º for 20-22 minutes.

SALTED BEER CARAMEL

This recipe is so good it actually drove the OMC to create the toffee bundt cake recipe around it. Bent Paddle beer adds a subtle maltiness and character to a deeply sweet sauce.

Yield: 4 Cups

Ingredients
4 cups white cane sugar
1 cup Bent Paddle Cold Press beer or other coffee beer
1 cup butter
2 cups heavy cream
2 tsp sea salt

Instructions
In a LARGE pot (caramel will bubble up to 10x its original volume, so you're looking for at least a 10 quart pot), add sugar and beer. Mix well. Place pot over high heat and stir until the sugar has melted, then stop stirring. Near the end of the cooking process, the caramel will reduce back down in size. Allow to boil untouched until the caramel reaches a deep amber color. Once caramel is ready, heat heavy cream to a boil in a separate pan. Slowly whisk the cream and salt into the sugar mixture. Return mixture to heat and cook until slightly thickened (about 3 minutes). Remove from heat, stir in butter, and allow to cool before transferring into a container.

Bent Paddle is among Duluth's best micro breweries, just down the street from OMC. Their beer finds a place in both the ESB Barbecue sauce and this delicious caramel.

Salted Beer Caramel

Toffee Bundt Cake

We often send ice cream lovers across the street to Love Creamery. It's a hip shop with unique flavors and even some creative milk alternatives like sunflower or oat.

"This is definitely a down south cake," Jaima says. "It wasn't as easy to create or get people to try it because it's fairly complex. But it got some great momentum."

Yield: 8-16 Pieces

Ingredients
Cake
3 cups all-purpose flour, plus more for pans
2 cups granulated sugar
1 teaspoon salt
1 teaspoon baking soda
1 teaspoon ground cinnamon
3 large eggs, beaten
1 ½ cups vegetable oil
1 ½ teaspoons vanilla extract
1 8 oz can crushed pineapple (don't drain)
2 cups chopped ripe bananas
   (about 3 bananas)
1 cup chopped pecans, toasted
Crisco for greasing

Frosting
2 8 oz packages cream cheese, softened
1 cup salted butter or margarine, softened
2 16 oz package powdered sugar
2 teaspoons vanilla extract
¾ cup pecans, crumbled
   and toasted

Instructions
Mix first five ingredients in bowl, add eggs and oil, and blend until just moistened. Stir in vanilla, pineapple, bananas, and pecans. Preheat oven to 350º. Grease and flour three 9-inch round cake pans and pour in the batter.

Bake 25–30 minutes or until a wooden toothpick inserted in center comes out clean. Cool completely (about an hour).

It's frosting time. Beat cream cheese and butter until smooth (medium-low speed on an electric mixer). Add in powdered sugar a little at a time, mixing at low speed to incorporate after each addition. Stir in vanilla, beat until fluffy.

Assemble cake. Put down one layer, spread with a cup of frosting. Top with the second layer, repeat. Top with third layer, spread remaining frosting over the top and sides, and arrange pecans liberally over the whole thing. There's also no rule against using more pecans if you're into that.

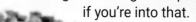

BISCUITS

Flaky perfection! Freeze the butter, don't overwork the dough, use a light touch. Wrong. Not light enough. Work it even less next time. When you get it right, fluffy like a cloud...It's so worth it.

Modern American "biscuits" are actually a form of scones. In their earliest form, they likely came from Scotland, where oat and barley flour mixed with liquid and fat were cooked on griddles and cut into wedges. They've only gotten lighter and flakier since then, to everyone's benefit.

Yield: 9 Large Biscuits

Ingredients
4 cups all-purpose flour
2 cups buttermilk
1½ sticks of butter (frozen)
2 Tbsp baking powder
2 tsp salt
1/2 tsp baking soda

Instructions
Shred frozen butter with a cheese grater, re-freeze. Combine dry ingredients in a bowl. Add frozen butter to flour mix. Add buttermilk and mix until combined. (**Do not overwork dough**).

Place the dough onto a floured table. Push the dough out until it's about 1/2 inch thick. Fold dough and pat down until 1 inch thick. Repeat for a total of 4 folds.

Preheat oven to 375º. Cut out biscuits, spray half sheet with pan spray and place biscuits on sheet tray, slightly touching each other. Brush tops with olive oil. Bake in oven for 18–20 minutes at 375°.

The gravy is rich, the biscuits are flaky. I'm sorry you can't eat this photo.

A traditional cornbread with some extra sweetness, this straddles the border between bread and cake. Buttermilk gives it moisture and richness.

**Yield:
9X9 Pan**

Ingredients
1 cup flour
1 cup cornmeal
2 tsp baking powder
1 tsp salt
1 large egg
1/4 cup granulated sugar
1/4 cup honey
1 cup buttermilk
1 stick melted butter

Instructions
Preheat oven to 350°. Grease 9x9 cake pan (we show cast iron because it looks cool, but you will probably find it easier to just use a regular cake pan or a glass pie dish). Sprinkle with cornmeal to prevent sticking (or use Pam if you're feeling lazy).

Mix flour, cornmeal, baking powder, and salt in large bowl. Whisk. Mix sugar, honey, buttermilk, and egg in separate bowl. Whisk.

Create well in dry ingredients and pour in wet mixture. Fold until combined. Once combined, pour in melted butter and continue to fold until thick batter forms. (Some lumps okay). Do not overmix. Pour batter into the pan and bake at 350° 25-30 minutes, or until toothpick inserted in the middle comes out clean and cornbread bounces back when touched.

Adding whole kernel corn, jalapeños, or bits of leftover brisket to your cornbread can make delightful variations.

As mentioned above, you can cook this recipe in any number of baking pan types

What Makes a Good Home Smoker?

Hollywood has taught us that you don't succeed by having the best tools or throwing money at a problem. Instead, what matters is grit. Unfortunately, in barbecue? You want the best tools. And you're going to end up throwing money at the problem.

"It's not really the cook so much that matters, it's the cooker," Red Wagon BBQ owner Joe Slack explains. "It's gotta be designed properly and it's gotta hold the heat right."

What Joe means is "wood-fired". OMC partner Jeff Petcoff, though, thinks the situation is not so black and white.

"I'd say there's a whole spectrum of what's acceptable and what's not," Jeff says. "There's some pure hearted people who say wood-fired all the way. You just can't do that in Northern Minnesota."

Expensive Smoker (Stick Burner)

"I think the first thing people want to realize is: the thicker the metal in their smoker, the better result they're going to get," Joe says. His setup has 1/4 inch steel walls, which are thick and hold heat extremely well. Plan to spend $500 or $600 on a small but heavy duty home unit. Joe spent $5000 on his! (It holds 10 briskets).

"For somebody who wants to smoke something occasionally," Joe says. "It does make it a lot easier."

Electric/Gas Smoker

Now we'll get controversial. Joe Slack says for true Central Texas style barbecue, a modern pellet smoker rarely gets the job done.

A *Southern Pride* smoker, model SPK-500 Mobile

"You can get barbecue out of wood chips, but it won't be like you get it in Central Texas," Joe says. "The big boxes people use, they don't require as much attention. It doesn't have the consistency or flavor."

But for some home cooks, that may be exactly right. There are a lot of routes to the same goal and some are easier than others.

"We use a Southern Pride smoker. It's wood and propane heated; ideal for smoking high volume barabecue outside in freezing Minnesota winters," Jeff says. "That's something we picked up from the Plowboys in Kansas City. Q39 was another place we stopped. Those guys had Southern Pride smokers everywhere."

The Backyard Smoker

There *is* something to be said for the thickness of a smoker. Joe says if you save money on a $200 smoker with thin walls, you're setting yourself up for a lot of frustration later.

"The thin metal ones you get from the big box stores, they lose heat very easily and they're hard to regulate," Joe says.

The only exception is if you're obsessive to the point where you're truly well practiced. Joe's brother has a thin-walled New Braunfels smoker which he's learned to get great results out of. The problem was the learning curve.

"He's been smoking for probably 30 or 40 years," Joe says. "He probably cooks something daily."

At the end of the day, barbecue is a lifelong pursuit. You could test the waters with a simple model and risk irregular results, then upgrade to a thicker gauge smoker later. You could save time with a self-feeding electric model, realizing that there's an art to wood-fired you may be missing out on. Or you could convert an old propane tank into a smoker and really dive in. Ultimately, it's a choose-your-own adventure.

"If you have less time, you want an electric one with self-feeding pellets and a wide variety of woods to play with," Jeff says. "If you're more experienced, get your buddies to help you build one and sit there all day long. There's no wrong answer." OMC

Joe recommends: *Texas Longhorn BBQ Pits* in Uvalde, (model TL-17 shown above) or *Texas Lang BBQ Smokers* from Nanhunta, Georgia

What Makes Good Smoking Wood?

Barbecue is intensely regional. From the sauce to the protein, where you come from affects what you serve (Wyoming even has a tradition of barbecued mutton... not that the OMC goes quite that far). The OMC didn't want hickory, because that's a southern wood. Pecan is southern as well.

"We wanted to use something local that would represent our world," Louis says.

So they use pine. Just kidding.

Actually, they use oak and sugar maple from Lake Wood Designs, a small business a couple blocks down the road. The firewood is kiln-dried to remove moisture. This makes it burn cleaner, hotter, and more efficiently. Oak is hardwood that grows further north, and provides the dominant flavor in whiskey and some chardonnays. Wines made with oak may be described with terms like "caramel", "cream", or "spice". Sugar maple is even more iconically Minnesotan. It's mild and slightly sweet, with buttery, vanilla-like notes.

Finding good smoking wood isn't always straightforward. The Internet is one option and sometimes stores like Home Depot will sell smoking wood. But going to a barbecue place nearby and asking them for their source may be the best way to find the unadvertised deals. Know a guy who knows a guy? If his name is Jim and he works out of his backyard, he probably doesn't have a website.

Wherever you source it, finding the right wood makes a difference to the finished product. Hickory and mesquite provide a strong, potent flavor for quick smokes. Pecan, apple, or cherry are more mild for longer-duration smoking. Try a variety and see what you like best.

"The terroir of the wood is a big thing," Jeff says. "Minnesota's never been known as a barbecue hotspot, but hopefully, someday, it will be put on the map as a destination. The stylings will continue to develop." OMC

ACKNOWLEDGMENTS

Writing a cookbook is hard, but starting and running a restaurant is vastly harder. I first want to thank Tom, Jaima, Louis, Jeff, Dan and the rest of the OMC gang. Without them, there wouldn't be an OMC Smokehouse, and therefore also no OMC Cookbook.

As far as the book itself, I want to thank Rolf for his excellent photography. Rolf is semi-retired from photography but is still willing to do these books, and we really appreciate that. I also want to thank designer Rick, who has gone through many, many revisions with me. Tobbi, you are a good printer. Emma, you were really helpful in promoting this thing and helping with Indiegogo/Facebook/fundraising stuff.

I have to thank our two proofreaders: my wife Alicia and my mom Jayne. I mean, I appreciate other things about them as well, but in this context I appreciate their proofreading most. I am also thankful for my 3 and 5 year old daughters. They didn't do much, but they enjoy seeing their names in print: "Ruby". "Moo Moo." Look! Your names are in papa's book.

Finally, I want to thank the customers of the OMC and particularly the ones who picked up this book. You are the reason the restaurant exists, and I know everyone there is so thankful you keep coming and dining. Give yourselves a high five…and then a brisket sandwich.

Robert J Lillegard

Robert Lillegard
September 8, 2020

INDEX

14º ESB Barbecue Sauce, *9**, 11

A
Aioli, Malt Vinegar, 15, *29, 92*
Alabama White Sauce, *9,* 10

Appetizers
Jalapeño Brisket Bombs, 40, *40*
Pork Belly Lettuce Wraps, *37,* 41, *41*
Salmon Pimento Dip, 42, *42*
Smoked Chicken Quesadilla, 39, *39*
Super Nachos, 38, *38*

B

Bacon
Bacon and Blue Cheese Potato Salad, *21,* 26, *26*
Collard Greens, *21,* 22
Corn Relish, 30, *30*
Henny Penny, 82, *82*
Jalapeño Brisket Bombs, 40, *40*
Kentucky Hot Brown, 85
Loaded Mac and Cheese, 68, *68*
Smoked Chicken Club Wrap, 81, *81*

Bacon Fat
Bacon and Blue Cheese Potato Salad, *21,* 26, *26*

C
Collard Greens, *21,* 22
Country Gravy, 16

Baked Goods & Desserts
Biscuits, 111, *111*
Cornbread, 112, *112*
Hummingbird Cake, *107,* 110, *110*
Salted Beer Caramel, 109, *109*
Toffee Bundt Cake, 109, *109*
Whoopie Pie, 108, *108*
Balsamic Dressing, *13,* 14
Bama Brisket Wrap, 72, *72*

Barbecue
choosing a good home smoker, *113–14,* 113–15
choosing a good smoking wood, 116
ingredient sourcing, 105–06
research and travels, 43–46
thoughts on, 1–2

Barbecue Sauces. *See also* **Sauces & Dressings**
14º ESB Barbecue Sauce, *9,* 11
Alabama White Sauce, *9,* 10
Chipotle Cilantro Barbecue Sauce, *9,* 11, *11*
Georgia Gold Barbecue Sauce, *9,* 10
Honey Barbecue Sauce, *9,* 10
Korean Barbecue Sauce, *9,* 12, *12*
BBQ Ranch Salad, 81, *81*

Beans and Legumes
OMC Beans, *21,* 22
Vegetarian Sloppy Joe, 95, *95*

*Italicized numbers refer to photos

Beef

about, 63

cooking instructions for smoking a brisket, 64–67, *64–67*

sourcing, 105–06

Bama Brisket Wrap, 72, *72*

Brisket and Cheddar, 70, *70*

Haystack Brisket, 71, *71*

Jalapeño Brisket Bombs, 40, *40*

Loaded Mac and Cheese, 68, *68*

OMC Beans, *21*, 22

OMC Burger, *73*, *73*

OMC Tacos, 69, *69*

Beer

14° ESB Barbecue Sauce, *9*, 11

Salted Beer Caramel, 109, *109*

beverages. See cocktails

Bigelow, Valerie, 2, 88

Biscuits, 111, *111*

blue cheese

Bacon and Blue Cheese Potato Salad, *21*, 26, *26*

Blue Cheese Dressing, *13*, 14, *78*

Bourdain, Anthony, 1

Bowls

Korean BBQ Pork Belly Soba Noodle Bowl, 62, *62*

Smoked Pork Burrito Bowl, 58, *58*

Brisket

cooking instructions, 64–67, *64–67*

Bama Brisket Wrap, 72, *72*

Brisket and Cheddar, 70, *70*

Brisket Rub, *5*, 7

Haystack Brisket, 71, *71*

Jalapeño Brisket Bombs, 40, *40*

Loaded Mac and Cheese, 68, *68*

OMC Beans, *21*, 22

OMC Tacos, 69, *69*

Burger, OMC, 73, *73*

Burger Seasoning, *5*, 7

C

Cabbage

Classic Coleslaw, *21*, 23, *23*

Jalapeño Lime Slaw, *21*, 28

Korean BBQ Pork Belly Soba Noodle Bowl, 62, *62*

Cake

Hummingbird Cake, *107*, 110, *110*

Toffee Bundt Cake, 109, *109*

Candied Sweet Potato Bake, *21*, 25, *25*

Caramel, Salted Beer, 109, *109*

Catfish

Catfish Rub, *5*, 6, *6*

Catfish Sandwich, 94, *94*

Fried Catfish, 93, *93*

Cheddar Cheese

BBQ Ranch Salad, 81, *81*

Brisket and Cheddar, 70, *70*

Cheese Sauce, 17

Cheesy Jalapeño Grits, *21*, 24, *24*

Henny Penny, 82, *82*

Pork N' Grits, 57, *57*

Quesadilla, Smoked Chicken, 39, *39**

Salmon Pimento Dip, 42, *42*

Cheese

BBQ Ranch Salad, 81, *81*

Blue Cheese Dressing, *13*, 14, *78*

Brisket and Cheddar, 70, *70*

Cheese Sauce, 17

Cheesy Jalapeño Grits, *21*, 24, *24*

Elotes Dressing, *21*, 23, *23*

Henny Penny, 82, 82

Kentucky Hot Brown, 85

Mac and Cheese, Loaded, 68, *68*

Nachos, Super, 38, *38*

Peas and Pancetta, *21*, 27, *27*

Pork N' Grits, 57, *57*

Quesadilla, Smoked Chicken, 39, *39*

Salmon Pimento Dip, 42, *42*

Zip A Dee Do Da, 61, *61*

Chicken

about, 75

cooking instructions, 76–80, *76–80*

sourcing, 106

BBQ Ranch Salad, 81, *81*

Chicken Marinade, 76, *76*

Chicken Rub, 5, 6

Chicken Tender Dip and Dredge, 77–78, *77–78*

Chicken/Turkey Stacker, 85, *85*

Georgia Gold Sandwich, 84, *84*

Henny Penny, 82, 82

Kentucky Hot Brown, 85

Nashville Hot Chicken, 83, *83*

Nashville Hot Chicken Rub, *5*, 7

OMC Beans, *21*, 22

Smoked Chicken Club Wrap, 81, 81

Smoked Chicken Quesadilla, 39, *39*

Smoked Chicken Wings, 79, *79*

Whole Smoked Chicken, 80, *80*

Chipotle Cilantro Barbecue Sauce, *9*, 11, *11*

Cilantro

Chipotle Cilantro Barbecue Sauce, *9*, 11, *11*

Elotes Dressing, *21*, 23, *23*

Jalapeño Lime Slaw, *21*, 28

Citrus. *See* **lemons; limes**

Cluck. *See* **Chicken**

Cocktails

and ice, 101

inventing new, 100

the proper ratios, 100

technique, 101

Karin's Kup (Mezcal Margarita with Vermouth), 98

Kentucky Gold Rush, 102, *102*

Margarita, 101, *101*

N/A Lemonade, 104, *104*

Old Fashioned, 100, *100*

Red Sangria, 103, *103*

Watermelon Gin, 99, *99*

Coleslaw, Classic, *21*, 23, *23*

Collard Greens, 21, 22

Corn

Corn Relish, 30, *30*

Elotes Dressing, *21*, 23, *23*

Cornbread, 112, *112*

cornmeal, yellow

Cheesy Jalapeño Grits, *21*, 24, *24*

Cornbread, 112, *112*

*Italicized numbers refer to photos

Cotija Cheese

Elotes Dressing, *21*, 23, *23*

Country Gravy, 17

Cranberries

Rhubarb and Cranberry Jam, 14, *14*

Cream Cheese

Hummingbird Cake, *107*, 110, *110*

Jalapeño Brisket Bombs, 40, *40*

Salmon Pimento Dip, 42, *42*

Cured, Braised, Smoked and Fried Pork
Belly, 55–56, *55–56*

D

Desserts & Baked Goods

Biscuits, 111, *111*

Cornbread, *112, 112*

Hummingbird Cake, *107*, 110, *110*

Salted Beer Caramel, 109, *109*

Toffee Bundt Cake, 109, *109*

Whoopie Pie, 108, *108*

Dips and Spreads

Rhubarb and Cranberry Jam, 14, *14*

Salmon Pimento Dip, 42, *42*

Tomato and Black Pepper Jam, 12

The Duluth Grill, 33–36, 87

E

Elotes Dressing, *21*, 23, *23*

F

Fish

cooking instructions, 90–91, *90–91*

Catfish, Fried, 93, *93*

Catfish Rub, *5*, 6

Catfish Sandwich, 94, *94*

Salmon Pimento Dip, 42, *42*

Smoked Salmon, *90*–91, *90–91*

Smoked Salmon Wrap, 92, *92*

Franklin BBQ (Austin), 45, *45*

French Dressing, *13*, 15, *15*

French Fries, 29, *29*

Fried Catfish, 93, *93*

G

Georgia Gold Barbecue Sauce, *9*, 10

Georgia Gold Sandwich, 84, *84*

Gouda cheese

Cheese Sauce, 17

Cheesy Jalapeño Grits, *21*, 24, *24*

Gravy

Country Gravy, 16

Hot Brown Gravy, 17, *17*

Greens, Collard, *21*, 22

Grits

Cheesy Jalapeño Grits, *21*, 24, *24*

Pork N' Grits, 57, *57*

H

Hanson, Ashley, *iv*, 44, 88

Hanson, Jaima, *iv*, 1, 2, 18–20, *19*, 33–34,
43–45, 87–88, *88*

Hanson, Louis, *iv*, 1–2, 34, *34*, 36, 43–44,
46, 87–88, 88, 105–06

Hanson, Tom, *iv*, 1, 2, 8, 18, 33–34, 34,
43–46, 87–88

Haystack Brisket, 71, *71*

Haystack Onions, 28, *28*

Henny Penny, 82, *82*

Honey

Georgia Gold Barbecue Sauce, *9*,* 10

Honey Barbecue Sauce, *9*, 10

my wife Alicia, v, 117

hospitality, 18–20

Hot Brown, Kentucky, 85

Hot Brown Gravy, 16, *16*

Hummingbird Cake, *107*, 110, *110*

J

Jalapeños

Cheesy Jalapeño Grits, *21*, 24, *24*

Elotes Dressing, *21*, 23, *23*

Jalapeño Brisket Bombs, 40, *40*

Jalapeño Business, 16, *16*

Jalapeño Lime Slaw, *21*, 28

Pickled Jalapeños, 32, *32*

Jam

Rhubarb and Cranberry Jam, 14, *14*

Tomato and Black Pepper Jam, 12

Johns, Todd, 45

K

Karin's Kup (Mezcal Margarita with Vermouth), 98

Kentucky Gold Rush, 102, *102*

Kentucky Hot Brown, 85

Korean Barbecue Sauce, *9*, 12, *12*

Korean BBQ Pork Belly Sandwich, 60, *60*

Korean BBQ Pork Belly Soba Noodle Bowl, 62, *62*

L

"Larry's" Seasoning Salt, *5*, 7

LeFebvre, Dan, *iv*, 34, 43–44, *44*, 46

Lemons

N/A Lemonade, 104, *104*

Lentils

Vegetarian Sloppy Joe, 95, *95*

Lewis, John, Jr., 46

Limes

Elotes Dressing, *21*, 23, *23*

Jalapeño Lime Slaw, *21*, 28

M

Mac and Cheese, Loaded, 68, *68*

Mains

Bama Brisket Wrap, 72, *72*

BBQ Ranch Salad, 81, *81*

Brisket and Cheddar, 70, *70*

Catfish, Fried, 93, *93*

Catfish Sandwich, 94, *94*

Chicken/Turkey Stacker, 85, *85*

Cured, Braised, Smoked and Fried Pork Belly, 55–56, *55–56*

Georgia Gold Sandwich, 84, *84*

Haystack Brisket, 71, *71*

Kentucky Hot Brown, 85

Korean BBQ Pork Belly Sandwich, 60, *60*

Korean BBQ Pork Belly Soba Noodle Bowl, 62, *62*

Loaded Mac and Cheese, 68, *68*

Nashville Hot Chicken, 83, *83*

Northern Pride, 59, *59*

OMC Burger, 73, *73*

OMC Tacos, 69, *69*

Pork Butt, 48–50, *48–50*

*Italicized numbers refer to photos

Pork N' Grits, 57, *57*

Pulled Pork, 51–52, *51–52*

Smoked Chicken Club Wrap, 81, *81*

Smoked Pork Burrito Bowl, 58, *58*

Smoked Salmon Wrap, 92, *92*

St. Louis Style Pork Ribs, 53–54, *53–54*

Vegetarian Sloppy Joe, 95, *95*

Malt Vinegar Aioli, 15, *29*, 92

Margarita, 101, *101*

Mayonnaise

Alabama White Sauce, *9*, 10

Bacon and Blue Cheese Potato Salad, *21, 26, 26*

Blue Cheese Dressing, *13*, 14, *78*

Elotes Dressing, *21*, 23, *23*

Malt Vinegar Aioli, 15, *29*, 92

Ranch Dressing, *13*, 15, *15*

Mezcal Margarita with Vermouth (Karin's Kup), 98

Moo. *See* **Beef**

Moo Moo, 117

Mushrooms

Loaded Mac and Cheese, 68, *68*

Mustard

14° ESB Barbecue Sauce, *9*, 11

Georgia Gold Barbecue Sauce, *9*, 10

N

Nachos, Super, 38, *38*

N/A Lemonade, 104, *104*

Nashville Hot Chicken, 83, *83*

Nashville Hot Chicken Rub, *5*, 7

Noodles. *See* **soba noodles**

Northern Pride, 59, *59*

Nuts

Candied Sweet Potato Bake, *21*, 25, *25*

Hummingbird Cake, *107*, 110, *110*

O

Oink. *See* **Pork**

Old Fashioned, 100, *100*

OMC Beans, *21*, 22

OMC Burger, 73, *73*

OMC Smokehouse

building restoration, *33–36*, 36

ingredient sourcing, 105–06

the name, 8

perfect *vs.* good enough philosophy, 4

research and travels, 43–46

restaurant history, 33–36

smoker and smoking wood choices, *113–16*, 113–16

OMC Tacos, 69, *69*

Onions

Brined Onions, 31, *31*

Haystack Onions, 28, *28*

P

Pancetta, Peas and, *21*, 27, *27*

Pappy's (St. Louis), 45

Parmesan Cheese

Hot Brown Gravy, 17, *17*

Kentucky Hot Brown, 85

Peas and Pancetta, *21*, 27, *27*

Pasta

Loaded Mac and Cheese, 68, *68*

Peas and Pancetta, *21*, 27, *27*

Pecans

Candied Sweet Potato Bake, *21, 25, 25**

Hummingbird Cake, *107*, 110, *110*

Pepper Jack cheese

Zip A Dee Do Da, 61, *61*

Petcoff, Jeff, *iv*, 34, *34*, 36, 43–44, *46*, 87, 88, 113–15, 116

Pickles

Brined Onions, 31, *31*

Pickled Jalapeños, 32, *32*

Pollan, Michael, 1

Pork

about, 47

cooking instructions, 48–56, *48–56*

sourcing, 105

Northern Pride, 59, *59*

OMC Beans, *21*, 22

OMC Burger, 73, *73*

Pork Butt, 48–50, *48–50*

Pork N' Grits, 57, *57*

Pork Rub, 5, 6, *6*

Pulled Pork, 51–52, *51–52*

Smoked Pork Burrito Bowl, 58, *58*

St. Louis Style Pork Ribs, 53–54, *53–54*

Super Nachos, 38, *38*

Zip A Dee Do Da, 61, *61*

Pork Belly

cooking instructions, 55–56, *55–56*

Cured, Braised, Smoked and Fried Pork Belly, 55–56, *55–56*

Korean BBQ Pork Belly Sandwich, 60, *60*

Korean BBQ Pork Belly Soba Noodle Bowl, 62, *62*

Pork Belly Lettuce Wraps, 37, 41, *41*

Potatoes

Bacon and Blue Cheese Potato Salad, *21*, 26, *26*

banana, v, 117

French Fries, 29, *29*

Pulled Pork, 51–52, *51–52*

Q

Q39 (Kansas City), 45–46

Quesadilla, Smoked Chicken, 39, *39*

Quinoa

Vegetarian Sloppy Joe, 95, *95*

R

Ranch Dressing, *13*, 15, *15*

Red Sangria, 103, *103*

Red Wagon BBQ (Waco), 46

Rhubarb and Cranberry Jam, 14, *14*

Ribs, St. Louis Style Pork, 53–54, *53–54*

Rice

Smoked Pork Burrito Bowl, 58, *58*

roasted red peppers

Salmon Pimento Dip, 42, *42*

Rubs

Brisket Rub, *5*, 7

Burger Seasoning, *5*, 7

Catfish Rub, *5*, 6

Chicken Rub, *5*, 6

"Larry's" Seasoning Salt, *5*, 7

Nashville Hot Chicken Rub, *5*, 7

Pork Rub, 5, 6, *6*

S

Salad, BBQ Ranch, 81, *81*

*Italicized numbers refer to photos

Salmon

about, 89

cooking instructions, 90–91, *90–91*

Salmon Pimento Dip, 42, *42*

Smoked Salmon, 90–91, *90–91*

Smoked Salmon Wrap, 92, *92*

Salted Beer Caramel, 109, *109*

Sandwiches

Bama Brisket Wrap, 72, *72*

Brisket and Cheddar, 70, *70*

Catfish Sandwich, 94, *94*

Chicken/Turkey Stacker, 85, *85*

Georgia Gold Sandwich, 84, *84*

Haystack Brisket, 71, *71*

Henny Penny, 82, *82*

Kentucky Hot Brown, 85

Korean BBQ Pork Belly Sandwich, 60, *60*

Nashville Hot Chicken, 83, *83*

Northern Pride, 59, *59*

OMC Burger, 73, *73*

Smoked Chicken Club Wrap, 81, *81*

Smoked Salmon Wrap, 92, *92*

Vegetarian Sloppy Joe, 95, *95*

Zip A Dee Do Da, 61, *61*

Sangria, Red, 103, *103*

Sauces & Dressings. *See also* **Barbecue Sauces**

Balsamic Dressing, *13,* 14

Blue Cheese Dressing, *13,* 14, *78*

Country Gravy, 16

Elotes Dressing, *21,* 23, *23*

French Dressing, *13,* 15, *15*

Hot Brown Gravy, 17, *17*

Jalapeño Business, 16, *16*

Malt Vinegar Aioli, 15, *29, 92*

Ranch Dressing, *13,* 15, *15*

Rhubarb and Cranberry Jam, 14

Soba Noodle Dressing, 16

Sausage

Country Gravy, 16

Sides

Bacon and Blue Cheese Potato Salad, *21,* 26, *26*

Candied Sweet Potato Bake, *21,* 25, *25*

Cheesy Jalapeño Grits, *21,* 24, *24*

Classic Coleslaw, *21,* 23, *23*

Collard Greens, *21,* 22

Corn Relish, 30, *30*

Elotes Dressing, *21,* 23, *23*

French Fries, 29, *29*

Haystack Onions, 28, *28*

Jalapeño Lime Slaw, *21,* 28

OMC Beans, *21,* 22

Peas and Pancetta, *21,* 27, *27*

Slack, Joe, 2, 44, 46, *46,* 113–15

Slaw

Classic Coleslaw, *21,* 23, *23*

Jalapeño Lime Slaw, *21,* 28

Sloppy Joe, Vegetarian, 95, *95*

Smoked Chicken, Whole, 80, *80*

Smoked Chicken Club Wrap, 81, *81*

Smoked Chicken Quesadilla, 39, *39*

Smoked Chicken Wings, 79, *79*

Smoked Pork Burrito Bowl, 58, *58*

Smoked Salmon, 90–91, *90–91*

Smoked Salmon Wrap, 92, *92*

Smokers

choosing a good home smoker, *113–15,* 113–15

choosing a good smoking wood, 116

Soba Noodles
Korean BBQ Pork Belly Soba Noodle Bowl, 62, *62*
Soba Noodle Dressing, 16

Sour Cream
Elotes Dressing, *21,* 23, *23*

Sriracha
Korean Barbecue Sauce, *9,* 12, *12*
St. Louis Style Pork Ribs, 53–54, *53–54*
Stuckey, Bobby, 18
Super Nachos, 38, *38*
Sweet Potato Bake, Candied, *21,* 25, *25*

T
Tacos, OMC, 69, *69*

Tamari
Korean Barbecue Sauce, *9,* 12, *12*
Soba Noodle Dressing, 16
Toffee Bundt Cake, 109, *109*

Tomatoes
OMC Beans, *21,* 22
Tomato and Black Pepper Jam, 12

Tortillas
Bama Brisket Wrap, 72, *72*
OMC Tacos, 69, *69*
Smoked Chicken Club Wrap, 81, *81*

Smoked Salmon Wrap, 92, *92*

Turkey
Chicken/Turkey Stacker, 85, *85*

V
Vegetarian Sloppy Joe, 95, *95*

W
Watermelon Gin, 99, *99*
Whole Smoked Chicken, 80, *80*
Whoopie Pie, 108, *108*
Wings, Smoked Chicken, 79, *79*
wood choices for smoking, 116

Wraps
Bama Brisket Wrap, 72, *72*
Smoked Chicken Club Wrap, 81, *81*
Smoked Salmon Wrap, 92, *92*

Z
Zip A Dee Do Da, 61, *61*